See Dick Cook
A Culinary Voyage for the Average Man

KELLY LABONTE

Copyright © 2014 Kelly Labonte

All rights reserved.

ISBN: 0993921701
ISBN-13: 978-0993921704

DEDICATION

This book is for my family and my boys. The support you've shown me through this entire process has been unwavering and I love you all for that. To my best friend Rachel, for your creative prowess and that offside sense of humor I love so much. And for my husband Reg, my favourite "Dick" of them all. Without your encouragement this book would have never seen a keystroke.

You are my rock.

WARNING!

THE FOLLOWING RECIPES
ARE COMPLETELY SUITABLE FOR ALL DICKS.
USER DISCRETION IS NOT ADVISED.

Table of Contents

DICK'S KIT 11
- Dick's Tool Box 12
- Dick's Staples 14
- Dick's Dictionary of Gastronomic Jargon 16
- Dick's Doneness Chart 21
- Dick Likes It Creamy Caesar Salad Dressing 22
- Dick's Cheater Garlic Butter 23
- Dick's Tzatziki Sauce 24
- Six Month Mari-Me-Nara Sauce 26
- Dick's Garlic Croutons 28
- Sultry Sour Cream 29

IT'S A GUY THING – SNACKS AND APP'S 30
- A Total Cheese Ball 31
- Bachelor Bites 32
- Bad Boy Bruschetta 34
- Cocktail Weenie's 36
- Crab Stuffed Popper Cherry Tomatoes 37
- Dick's Bread n' Butter 38
- Fromage et Trois Spinach Dip 40
- Good Shit Baked Brie 42
- I'm The Man Hamburgers with Sautéed Onions 44
- Love Slugs 46
- Nascar Nachos 48
- Pigs and Popper's 50
- Poker Pizza Dip 52
- Real Men Do Cry French Onion Soup 54
- Red Hot Red Pepper Soup 56
- Reservoir Dogs Casserole 58
- She's Perfect Pesto Portabellas 60
- Hot Mama Melts 61
- Single and Sexy Caesar Salad 62
- Sloppy Dicks 64

Smokin' Gouda Dip 66

  Stalker Soup 68

  The Super Bowl Cheese Fondue 70

  Wingman 72

GOING, GOING, GONE… 75

  Banger and Dash 76

  Bite Me Sheppard's Pie 78

  Blackened Sole 80

  Cold Shoulder, Hot Catfish 82

  A Swing and a Miss Chipotle Chicken 83

  Feeling Smothered Pasta 84

  It's Not Me, It's You Meatloaf 86

  Jerk-Off Chicken 88

  Let Her Down Easy Eggplant Parmesan 90

  One Crazy Taco 92

  ShishkaDicks 94

  Stick a Fork In It Porchetta Roast 96

  We're Better Off Friends Fettuccini 98

  Splitsville Pea Soup 100

COOKING WITH HOOCH 101

  Beer Me Cheddar Soup 102

  Chili on a Bender 104

  Ciao Bella Steak 106

  Crabby Chicks 108

  Fishing for Compliments 110

  French Liqueur Chicken 112

  I'm a Catch Chicken Marsala 114

  Marg Or Rita Chicken 116

  Mojo-Mojito Shrimp 118

  On Tap Guinness Stew 120

  Seducer Sambuca Shrimp and Scallops 122

  Slow Cooker Beef au Beer Sandwiches 124

  That's the Spirit Pork Tenderloin 126

 Thighs of Rum & Coconut 128

 Jacked Meat 130

BACK OF THE LINE BOYS...SHE'S ALL MINE 131

 Big Balls Spaghetti... 132

 Bombshell Burrito's 134

 Crazy Chick Salad 136

 Crème de la Femmes Salmon 138

 Flex Your Mussels 140

 Fromage et Deux Jumbo Shells 142

 Fuhgeddaboudit Prime Rib 144

 Hide the Salami Baked Chicken 146

 Honey I'm Home Pork Chops 148

 Man Up Sausage Manicotti 150

 Mari-Me-Nara Spaghetti with Meatballs and Sausage 152

 Nice Rack...of Lamb 154

 One at a Time Ladies Lasagna 156

 Tap That Sea Bass 158

 Throw Me a Bone Bake 'n Barbecue Ribs 160

MEET THE PARENTS 161

 A Bow Tie Event.. 162

 Penniless Beef Tenderloin 164

 Bagger Steak with Béarnaise Sauce 166

 Crazy About Her Clam and Linguine.. 168

 French Guy Meat Pie... 170

 Fruit of Their Loins Grilled Halibut & Mango Salsa 172

 Gobble It Up Turkey Casserole 174

 I'm Really Not a Jackass Jambalaya 176

 A Penne For Your Thoughts 178

 Keeping it Wrapped Grilled Jumbo Shrimp 180

 Meet the Chief Beef Stroganoff with Bacon 182

 Their Little Lamb Chops 184

 Who's Your Daddy Chicken Diablo 186

 Three Sheets to the Wind Chicken 188

What a Ham	190
Three Months' Salary My Ass Salmon	192

OFF SIDE 193

Asparadick and Hollandaise	194
Back in Black Bean Rice	196
Baked Tomato Tata's	198
Bare Naked Garlic Mashed Potatoes	199
Bitchin' Broccoli Salad	200
Corn off the Wagon	201
Carb-a-Palooza Potato Casserole	202
Dick's Own Barbecue Salad	204
Dirty Girl Rice	205
Ears Like Cauliflower Casserole	206
Gold Digger Scalloped Potatoes	208
Manly Macaroni Salad	210
Nice Yams	212
Pre-Nup Fried Zucchini	213
Seeing Red Potato Salad	214
She's So Sweet Potato Frites	216
Teaser Tomato and Cucumber Salad	218
Rice Peel-Off	219
Wicked Wedges	220
Wine and Cheese Biscuits	221

DICK'S KIT

Welcome to the beginning of your voyage Dick. This short chapter is going to get you all set to start 'working it' in the kitchen. In here we are going to let you know which basic tools of the trade you will need, a list of items for you to keep on hand and a basic list of terms and definitions for you to refer to in that moment of doubt.

"Humor keeps us alive. Humor and food. Don't forget food. You can go a week without laughing."
― Joss Whedon

DICK'S TOOL BOX

Every job needs a tool or two and every guy needs a fully equipped toolbox. The kitchen is no exception Dick. Here is a list of items that will have you prepared for your culinary voyage.

A half decent set of pots and pans including some non-stick ones

A good set of knives – this will save you hours of frustration

13" x 9" Baking Dish

Barbecue Cage

Casserole Dish Set (various sizes)

Digital Meat Thermometer

Dutch Oven (yes - this actually exists)

Electric Knife

Electric Mixer

Food Processor (an average sized one will do)

Grapefruit Spoon

Garlic Crusher (a hard-core one Dick, not cheap)

Heavy-duty Oven Proof Skillet

Measuring Cups

Measuring Spoons/Wooden Spoons

Meat Tenderizer

Metal Skewers

Oven Mitts – Manly ones

Pastry Brush

Rice Cooker

Roasting Pan

Roasting Pan Drip Rack

Salad Spinner

Salt and Pepper Mills

Sauce Pan

Slow Cooker / Crock Pot

Strainer/Colander

Timer (if you can't work the one on the microwave)

Whisk

DICK'S STAPLES

There will be certain items and ingredients that appear regularly throughout this book Dick. Keeping these items on hand will ensure you have the necessary ingredients for most recipes that you'll find in here. That, and it makes you look like you know what you're doing.

You're a professional Dick. Act like it.

All Purpose Flour

Bacon

Beef Broth

Beer (Yes – you cook with it too Dick)

Black Pepper – fresh peppercorns with a mill

Butter and/or Olive Oil Based Margarine

Chicken Broth

Chili Pepper Sauce

Cooking Onions and/or Spanish Onions

Cream Cheese

Dick's Garlic Butter

Dijon Mustard

Dry Red Wine - always

Dry White Wine – always

Eggs

Feta Cheese

Garlic - fresh

Italian Seasoned Bread Crumbs

Jar of Chopped garlic

Jasmine Rice

Lemon Juice

Lipton Onion Soup Mix (regular or garlic)

Mayonnaise (for the love of God – real Mayo)

Non-Stick Cooking Spray (Olive Oil Variety)

Olive Oil – Light

Parmesan Cheese

Pesto (Basil variety)

Red Wine Vinegar

Sage Seasoning

Sea Salt

Seasonings/Spices – Basil, Cayenne, Cajun, Cinnamon, Dill, Garlic Powder (not salt Dick – powder), Herbes de Provence, Montreal Steak Spice, Nutmeg, Onion Powder, Oregano, Paprika, Parsley Flakes, Red Pepper Flakes, Season Salt, Thyme, White Pepper

Shallots

Six Month Mari-Me-Nara Sauce (keep frozen in one and two cup portions)

Tabasco or other Hot Sauce

White Vinegar

Worcestershire Sauce

DICK'S DICTIONARY OF GASTRONOMIC JARGON

If you find yourself confused or unsure about some of the terminology used in the book, this reference guide will square you away with what it all means. I know you won't ask for directions Dick, so here they are.

Al Dente	This describes pasta cooked firm to the bite – in other words, not mushy.
Au jus	This is the natural drippings or juice from a pan after cooking beef and deglazing.
Baste	This is when you brush, squirt or pour drippings or liquid, over food while broiling, roasting or baking. It prevents your food from drying out and adds flavour with the cooking juices.
Beat	To mix foods thoroughly to a smooth, even consistency using a spoon, fork, whisk or electric beater/mixer.
Blackened	A method of cooking that uses spices to coat meat or fish and then cooked in a very hot cast iron skillet to 'blacken' the outside.
Blanch	To cook food briefly in boiling water.
Broil	A method of cooking where the food is placed directly underneath the source of high heat.
Broth	A flavourful liquid made by simmering meats, fish, poultry or bones in water with herbs. This is also referred to as Stock.
Brown	To quickly sear food to enhance and lock-in flavor. This is normally done at the beginning of the cooking process with meat.
Brush	To coat food with a liquid such as melted butter or a glaze using a brush designed for this process – or a pastry brush.
Combine	This simply means mixing ingredients together.

Cube	The process of cutting something up into bite sized pieces.
Dash	This is a very small amount of seasoning, about 1/16th of a teaspoon. Sometimes referred to as a pinch.
Deep-fry	To cook submerged in very hot fat or grease until golden brown.
Deglaze	To swirl a liquid into a pan to dissolve particles of food on the bottom and sides of the pan for flavor.
Demi-glace	A rich brown sauce made from reduced beef stock or broth.
Deseed	To remove the seeds out of a fruit or vegetable.
Devein	This is the process of removing the black thread-like track from the back of a shrimp or prawn with a small knife.
Dice	To cut into regular sized cubes in accordance with the desired size.
Dilute	This is when you thin a liquid or reduce the intensity of flavour by adding liquid.
Direct Heat	A grilling method of cooking where food is cooked directly over a flame or heat source.
Dissolve	To stir a substance into a liquid until no solids remain.
Drain	This is simply to remove and discard the liquid contents from a cooking process.
Dredge	To lightly coat food to be pan-fried or sautéed. This is usually a breading of some sort.
Drippings	These are the juices and fat that is collected from the pan of cooked foods, such as roasts.
Dutch Oven	A large, deep pot that is covered with a tight fitting lid.
Filet	A boneless, skinless piece of meat.
Fillet	The process of removing the bones from fish or meat before cooking.

Flake	To break or flake food into small pieces.
Flambé	A method of cooking in which foods are splashed with liquor and ignited. Nice.
Garnish	This is a decorative touch added to dishes and beverages to enhance the appearance of the dish.
Glaze	A liquid that gives a shiny surface to an item, as in a glazed ham.
Grate	The process of shredding food into fine pieces.
Gratin	To sprinkle an item with cheese and/or bread crumbs and bake until golden brown.
Gravy	A sauce made from pan drippings and then thickened.
Grease	o cover a pan or dish with butter or oil to prevent food from sticking.
Grill	To cook directly over a heat source on metal racks – such as the barbecue.
Kebab	Small chucks of meat and vegetables skewered before cooking. Also called "shish kebab"
Knead	To press and fold dough in order to give it a smoother consistency needed for even cooking.
Marinade	A sauce that is used to soften and flavor meats before cooking.
Marinate	To soak meat, chicken or fish in a flavoured liquid mixture to enhance flavour and tenderness.
Medallion	A small piece of meat cut into an oval or a round shape.
Mince	To chop into very fine pieces, such as garlic.
Oven Bake	Cooking food surrounded by hot dry air in the oven.
Oven Broil	Cooking food with direct heat from above.

Pan Broil	Cooking food in a heavy pan without added fat and removing any fat that is produced as you cook the item.
Pan Fry	Cooking in a moderate amount of fat or oil, uncovered.
Parboil	To boil a food until it is partially cooked.
Pinch	A measurement of less than 1/16th of a teaspoon. Sometimes referred to as a dash.
Poach	To cook a food by placing it in a pot of simmering liquid.
Precook	To partially cook food before the final cooking process.
Preheat	To heat an oven to the recommended temperature before cooking in it.
Puree	The action of mashing a food until it has a thick, smooth consistency; usually done with a blender or food processor.
Reduce	To thicken and intensify the flavour of a liquid by boiling until the liquid reduces in volume, so the flavour is concentrated.
Roast	To cook foods by surrounding them with hot, dry air in an oven or over an open fire.
Sauté	To cook food in a small amount of butter or oil over a high heat in a shallow pan, so that it cooks and colours evenly.
Sear	To brown meat over a high temperature very quickly in order to seal in the juices.
Season	To improve the flavour of food by adding salt, pepper and other spices and flavours.
Shuck	To remove the shells from clams and oysters.
Sift	The process of removing lumps from certain foods while aerating it.
Simmer	To cook a pot or pan of food just below boiling point.

Skim	To remove fat or impurities that have risen to the top of a liquid being cooked.
Steam	To cook food by direct contact with steam.
Stew	To cook ingredients in a pot, gradually over a longer period of time.
Stir	To mix the entire contents of a bowl or saucepan to combine ingredients completely.
Stir-fry	Food that is cooked over a high heat with a small amount of in a pan or wok. The food is usually cut in small pieces to ensure quick cooking.
Strain	To separate the liquid contents from the solid food such as straining the liquid from the bones for stock.
Whisk	To mix using a whisk, fork or beater, to smoothly blend ingredients, or to incorporate as much air as possible into the mixture so it is light and airy.
Zest	The outer, coloured part of the peel of citrus fruit – usually grated from the fruit.

DICK'S DONENESS CHART

MEAT	BLUE *Cold and very red – soft and squishy*	RARE *Cold red center and soft to touch*	MEDIUM RARE *Warm red center and slightly soft*	MEDIUM *Pink and firm – hot throughout*	MEDIUM WELL *A hint of pink in the center - hot*	WELL *No pink at all and firm*
BEEF & VEAL	100° F	125° F	135° F	145° F	155° F	160° F
LAMB		135° F	145° F	160° F	165° F	170° F
PORK				160° F	165° F	170° F
POULTRY						175° F
GROUND MEAT						160° F
GROUND POULTRY						165° F

Remember Dick – meat will continue to cook for several minutes after it is removed from heat. To prevent overcooking, you will want to remove your beef slightly before it reaches the desired temperature.

Dick Likes It Creamy Caesar Salad Dressing

Absolutely the easiest, tastiest Caesar salad dressing you've ever had. Keep a batch of this on hand.

1 jar	Hellman's Mayonnaise	2 tbsp	Balsamic vinegar
4 tbsp	Parmesan cheese	½ tsp	Parsley
4 cloves	Garlic, minced	2 tbsp	Milk
2 tbsp	Red wine vinegar		

Procedure

Combine all ingredients in a bowl and mix well. Return the dressing mixture to the mayonnaise jar for use with Caesar salad and other recipes.

Servings: 20

Dick's Difficulty Gauge: Very easy

Preparation Time: 10 minutes
Cooking Time:
Inactive Time: 1 hour
Total Time: 1 hour and 10 minutes

Dicks Tips

If you can find the squeeze bottle style of mayonnaise, this is a good choice for the dressing. It's easy to use, and you can differentiate between your regular mayo and your Caesar salad dressing. Always keep some on hand in the fridge. The dressing will keep for the life of the mayo. And whatever you do Dick, DO NOT substitute Miracle Whip or some other "mayonnaise type" dressing. Stick with the real stuff.

Dick's Cheater Garlic Butter

Make a batch of this garlic butter and keep in a plastic container in the fridge for garlic bread, croutons, or whatever the need may be.

1 cup	Becel Margarine	3 tbsp	Parmesan cheese
3 cloves	Garlic, crushed	2 tsp	Dried parsley

Procedure

Mix all ingredients together in a plastic storage container and let sit for at least two hours. Keep handy and use as required.

Servings: 12
Yield: 1 cup

Dick's Difficulty Gauge: Very easy

Preparation Time: 5 minutes
Cooking Time:
Total Time: 5 minutes

Dicks Tips

For a simpler version in a pinch, substitute the fresh garlic for 2 tablespoons of garlic powder. Make sure you don't mix this up with garlic salt however or your butter will be salty tasting. Also – shoot for the Olive Oil version of your Becel if you can find it.

Dick's Tzatziki Sauce

How do you pronounce tzatziki? No idea - ask a Greek guy. But man is it good as a spread or dip.

1 cup	Greek style plain yogurt	1 tbsp	Lemon juice
½ cup	Sour cream	2 cloves	Garlic, minced
1 lg	English cucumber, peeled, seeded, finely grated then drained	½ tsp	Sea salt
		¼ tsp	White pepper
2 tbsp	Olive oil		
2 tbsp	Fresh dill, chopped fine		

Procedure

Pretty simple stuff here Dick. Throw all of the ingredients in a bowl, and stir until well blended.

Refrigerate for at least two hours before serving, to allow all the flavours to blend. Stir once more before serving. All done.

Servings: 8
Yield: 2 cups

Dick's Difficulty Gauge: Very easy

Preparation Time: 20 minutes
Inactive Time: 2 hours
Total Time: 2 hours and 20 minutes

Dicks Tips

An English cucumber is the long skinny variety you see in the grocery store, as opposed to its shorter, girthier cousin. Peel the skin off then cut the cucumber in half lengthwise to scoop out the seeds. Take the two halves and grate them finely into a bowl then hand squeeze the excess moisture out before adding to the mix. This will prevent a runny dip.

Your Greek Yogurt will be found with all the other yogurt in the dairy section of the store. It's plain, thicker and generally better for you. If you can't find any, you can substitute regular plain yogurt in its place, but I suggest you just look harder.

Six Month Mari-Me-Nara Sauce

Aptly named Six Month Mari-Me-Nara Sauce due to the fact it took 6 months, a lot of alcohol and a little blackmail to get the recipe for this sauce. It's a fantastic base for any pasta dish calling for tomato sauce and it's called for in numerous recipes throughout this book.

2 tbsp	Butter		1 5.5oz	Can of tomato paste
2 tbsp	Olive oil		2 tbsp	Basil pesto (Classico is good)
2	Cooking onions finely chopped		2 tbsp	Herbs de Provence seasoning
8	Garlic cloves, crushed		3 tbsp	Coarse sea salt
2 28oz	Cans of plum tomatoes		1 tbsp	Ground black pepper

Procedure

Melt butter along with olive oil over medium heat in a large sauce pot.

Add chopped onion and sauté on medium heat for approximately 10 minutes, or until onions are soft. Stir in crushed garlic.

Blend both cans of tomatoes, including juice in a blender until smooth and then transfer to sauce pot.

Add tomato paste, pesto, Herbs de Provence, salt and pepper. Simmer uncovered over low heat for at least 1 hour, stirring occasionally to allow the tastes to fully come out. The longer the simmer, the better the flavour!

Servings: 8
Yield: Approximately 6 Cups

Dick's Difficulty Gauge: Easy

Preparation Time: 20 minutes
Cooking Time: 1 hour
Total Time: 1 hour and 20 minutes

Dicks Tips

What the hell is pesto and where do you find it? It's a paste like sauce normally made from fresh basil, garlic, olive oil, and parmesan cheese. It can be found at the grocery store where spaghetti sauces are located. Look near the top shelf Dick, as the jars are generally small. Pesto is also a Dick Staple so be sure to keep it on hand. This sauce is a sure fire hit Dick and can be used as a base sauce for most any pasta dish, or on the side as a dip with some fresh garlic bread.

Dick's Garlic Croutons

Man does not live by bread alone Dick, but this simple crouton recipe comes in very handy for use in salads or soups.

1 loaf French bread - preferably a day or two old, cut into bite sized cubes	Coarse sea salt
2 tsp Herbes de Provence	Black pepper
	¼ cup Garlic flavored olive oil

Procedure

Preheat oven to 425° F.

In a large bowl, combine your bread cubes with the Herbes de Provence and a light sprinkling of salt and pepper.

Take your garlic flavoured olive oil and lightly drizzle the bread cubes, tossing to coat.

Arrange on an un-greased cookie sheet and bake for 10 - 15 minutes or until lightly browned.

Remove from oven and allow to cool.

Store in an air-tight container until ready to use.

Servings: 8

Dick's Difficulty Gauge: Very easy

Oven Temperature: 425°F

Preparation Time: 5 minutes
Cooking Time: 15 minutes
Total Time: 20 minutes

Dicks Tips

Any left-over bread will do here Dick, so long as it isn't too dense and you don't want it too fresh. You can freeze these for a rainy day as well in Ziploc bags.

Sultry Sour Cream

Use this in your Bad Boy Bruschetta recipe, or as a dipping sauce for potato wedges and other appetizers.

2 cups	Sour cream	2 tsp	Coarse sea salt
4 cloves	Garlic, crushed	2 tsp	Pepper

Procedure

Mix all ingredients together and keep refrigerated until ready to use.

Servings: 10

Dick's Difficulty Gauge: Very easy

Preparation Time: 5 minutes
Cooking Time:
Inactive Time: 1 hour
Total Time: 1 hour and 5 minutes

Dicks Tips

You can make this once and it should keep for about three weeks. The longer it sits, the better it tastes!

IT'S A GUY THING – SNACKS AND APP'S

"It's absolutely unfair for women to say that guys only want one thing: sex. We also want food."
~ Jarod Kintz

A Total Cheese Ball

Easy on the cheesy lines Dick...actions speak louder than words.

2 pkgs	Cream cheese, room temperature	1 12oz pkg	Bacon bits
½ cup	Sharp cheddar cheese, grated	1 small	Red onion, finely chopped
¼ cup	Dried chives	1 tsp	Garlic powder

Procedure

In a medium sized bowl, combine all ingredients until thoroughly blended.

Using your hands (wash them first Dick), shape cheese mixture into a ball and place on a glass serving dish. Refrigerate for thirty minutes and you're ready to go. Serve with a selection of crackers, spread around the cheese ball.

Servings: 6

Dick's Difficulty Gauge: Very easy

Preparation Time: 15 minutes
Cooking Time:
Inactive Time: 30 minutes
Total Time: 45 minutes

Dicks Tips

Leave the cream cheese out on the counter for at least an hour to reach room temperature. You can also cook your own bacon if you prefer. Fry up about seven slices or so, chop them up and add them in.
The Dick Factor: This is a great dish around the holidays. Make the little guy festive looking by placing a sprig of holly or rosemary on the plate.

Bachelor Bites

Nothing says 'I'm a bachelor' like throwing bacon in everything you cook. These are quick, easy and crammed with cheese and bacon. Could life be any better?

8 slices	Bacon, cooked and chopped	1 4oz pkg	Goat cheese
1 lb	Button mushrooms	2	Shallots, chopped
1 8oz pkg	Cream cheese, room temperature	½ tsp	Garlic powder

Procedure

Preheat your oven to 375° F.

Chop your raw bacon into small pieces and cook over medium high heat in small frying pan. Drain off fat and place bacon bits in a small bowl lined with paper towel to soak up excess grease.

Take each mushroom and using a small spoon remove the stem, hollowing out a small portion to place the dip mixture. Rinse and place on a paper towel to dry off.

In a small mixing bowl, combine cream cheese, goat cheese, chopped shallots, garlic powder and bacon bits. Stir until well blended.

Using a small spoon, carefully fill each mushroom cap with the cream cheese mixture and place upright on a baking sheet.

Bake at 375° for 15 minutes, or until tops begin to brown. Serve immediately.

Servings: 6
Yield: 20 - 24

Dick's Difficulty Gauge: Easy

Oven Temperature: 375°F

Preparation Time: 40 minutes
Cooking Time: 15 minutes
Total Time: 55 minutes

Dicks Tips

Shelling out the mushrooms can be a little tricky Dick but you just need to exercise a little patience. If you happen to have a grapefruit spoon, that would make the process much easier. And another thing. The smaller button mushrooms make these real easy to eat, but you could always substitute larger mushrooms if you can't find any at the grocery store.

Bad Boy Bruschetta

Chicks dig bad boys Dick, and bad boys who can make a mean bruschetta even more. A perfect appetizer for a romantic dinner for two, or a party for four. You decide.

4	lg	Tomatoes
½	cup	Green onions, chopped into small pieces
¼	cup	Red onion, finely chopped
15		Green olives with pimento, finely chopped
¼	cup	Parmesan cheese
¼	cup	Extra Virgin olive oil
3	tbsp	Balsamic vinegar
4		Garlic cloves, crushed or finely chopped
1	tbsp	Dried oregano
2	tsp	Coarse or Kosher salt
2	tsp	Coarse ground pepper
1	cup	Dicks Sour Cream
1	cup	Feta cheese
1		Loaf of Focaccia or Ciabatta bread
		Dicks Homemade Garlic Butter

Procedure

In a large plastic container with lid, combine the tomatoes, onions, olives, parmesan cheese, olive oil, balsamic vinegar, garlic, oregano, salt and pepper. Mix well, cover and refrigerate for at least three hours. The longer this sits the better Dick. Stir mixture once every hour or so.

When ready to eat, crumble the feta cheese into a separate bowl and set aside. Preheat the oven to 400° F.

Slice your bread into single serving portions and brush with some Dicks Homemade Garlic Butter. Place on a cookie sheet and bake in the oven at 400° F until bread appears slightly toasted.

Remove and place bread into a serving basket or onto tray. Put bruschetta, sour cream and feta into their own bowls with spoons. Have guests spread the bread with the sour cream mixture, spoon on some Bruschetta and top with feta.

Servings: 6
Yield: 4 cups

Dick's Difficulty Gauge: Easy

Oven Temperature: 400°F

Preparation Time: 30 minutes
Cooking Time:
Total Time: 3 hours

Dicks Tips

No Dick Factor needed here pal. This recipe will truly make you a rock star. Make sure your tomatoes are ripe but firm, and make this ahead of time so that the ingredients can all marinate. If your tomatoes are too ripe and your bruschetta is soupy, just drain the excess liquids just before serving.

Cocktail Weenie's

Okay, I didn't even have to make up a name for these. Total gimme!

1 cup	Ketchup		1 tsp	Dijon mustard
½ cup	Brown sugar, packed		2	Garlic cloves, minced
1 tbsp	Vinegar		1 lb	Turkey or chicken wieners, cut into 1 inch pieces
2 tsp	Soy sauce			

Procedure

Combine ketchup, brown sugar, vinegar, soy sauce, mustard, and garlic in the crock pot.

Cover and cook on high for 1 hour, stirring occasionally.

Add wieners; stir to coat with sauce.

Cover and cook on low for 1½ hours, or until hot. Serve hot with toothpicks, from the crock pot.

Servings: 4

Dick's Difficulty Gauge: Very easy

Preparation Time: 10 minutes
Cooking Time: 2 hours and 30 minutes
Total Time: 2 hours and 40 minutes

Dicks Tips

Choosing a low fat healthier dog will make this dish much healthier. Go for the chicken or turkey varieties without compromising at all on taste.

Crab Stuffed Popper Cherry Tomatoes

You don't even need hydro for this one Dick. A nice side on a hot day, just scoop, stuff and enjoy!

20 large	Cherry tomatoes	½ tsp	Dried basil
½ lb	Crab meat, real or imitation	½ tsp	Salt
¼ cup	Cream cheese	½ tsp	Pepper
2 tbsp	Mayonnaise		

Procedure

Using a small knife, slice the top off of each tomato. Next, using small spoon, carefully scoop out the pulp and seeds.

Sprinkle lightly with salt, then place them upside down on a paper towel to dry. Allow to sit for approximately 20 minutes.

Chop or flake crab meat and mix thoroughly with the remaining ingredients. Again with the small spoon, carefully stuff the crab mixture into the tomatoes, and place face up on a serving plate.

Servings: 4
Yield: 20

Dick's Difficulty Gauge: Very easy

Preparation Time: 20 minutes
Cooking Time: 20 minutes
Total Time: 40 minutes

Dicks Tips

If you've got a grapefruit spoon handy, I would suggest you use this to shell out the tomatoes. These can also be made ahead of time and refrigerated until ready to serve.

Dick's Bread n' Butter

This roasted garlic bread recipe combines some simple ingredients with genuine roasted garlic to give it that authentic taste. Likely to repel vampires as an added bonus. You're welcome.

3		Garlic heads - tops sliced off	2 tbsp	Parmesan cheese
1	tbsp	Olive oil	1 tsp	Parsley flakes
1	cup	Unsalted butter	1 loaf	Baguette or bread of your choice
¼	cup	Olive oil		

Procedure

Preheat the oven to 350° F.

With a sharp knife slice the tops off of the garlic heads allowing the tip of each clove to be exposed. Place garlic on a baking sheet - exposed side up - and drizzle with olive oil. Bake until garlic is soft, about 30 minutes. Remove and cool until easy to handle.

Meanwhile, back at the farm - in a small bowl, combine the unsalted butter with the olive oil, parmesan cheese and parsley.

Squeeze the soft roasted garlic into a small bowl and mash the contents with a fork forming a paste. Add the mashed garlic to the butter mixture and mix together until well blended.

Allow mixture to sit for at least a half an hour or more if you have the time to allow the flavours to spread throughout the butter mixture.

Now you've got your butter Dick so we just need the bread. Grab your bread of choice - slice the loaf in half or into individual slices and butter the bread. Refrigerate the leftovers for next time, and there will be a next time.

Turn the broiler on in the oven and roast bread garlic side up for 5 - 7 minutes or until the top is browned.

Slice and serve immediately.

Servings: 6
Yield: 1 cup of garlic butter

Dick's Difficulty Gauge: Easy

Oven Temperature: 350°F

Preparation Time: 10 minutes
Cooking Time: 40 minutes
Inactive Time: 30 minutes
Total Time: 1 hour and 20 minutes

Dicks Tips

Get a little creative with your bread here Dick. While the baguette will work just fine, how about a nice rosemary focaccia bread? Explore at the bakery aisle and pick something a little off the beaten path.

Dick Factor: Serve with some warmed up Mari-Me-Nara sauce as a flavorful dip. They'll be asking for loaf number two.

Fromage et Trois Spinach Dip

Is there anything better than a hot threesome of cheesiness? Mmmm...Cheese.

1	pkg	Cream cheese - room temperature	1 dash	Worcestershire sauce
¼	cup	Freshly grated Parmesan cheese	1 tbsp	Finely chopped red pepper
1	tsp	Garlic powder	1	Finely chopped green onion
1	tsp	Herbes de Provence seasoning	½ pkg	Frozen chopped spinach, thawed and squeezed dry
		Cayenne pepper (just a pinch Dick)	½ cup	Shredded cheddar cheese

Procedure

Preheat your oven to 400° F Dick.

In a large mixing bowl, beat the cream cheese, parmesan cheese, garlic powder, Herbes de Provence, cayenne and Worcestershire with a hand held electric mixer until smooth.

Now add your red pepper and green onion and mix on med-low just to blend in.

Throw in your squeezed dry spinach and mix until blended.

Place the entire mixture into an oven proof baking dish and top with shredded cheddar.

Bake for approximately 20 minutes. You will see the cheese dip bubbling at the edges when it's done.

Serve with tortilla chips or baked pita wedges.

Servings: 4

Dick's Difficulty Gauge: Very easy

Oven Temperature: 400°F

Dicks Tips

Find yourself some good pita wedges as they taste the best with this dish. To serve, place a napkin on a small glass plate then rest the hot dish out of the oven onto the napkin. This will keep it from sliding around.

Good Shit Baked Brie

I struggled to name this dish for months when one night a fellow 'Dick' takes a bite and exclaims to a patio full of people, "This is good shit". Nope, can't top that.

1		Brie round (the size will depend on number of guests but an average one is good for 4 people)	1	tbsp	Butter or margarine
			3		Garlic cloves, chopped or minced
½	cup	Red peppers, chopped	½	tbsp	Montreal Steak Spice
2	med	Shallots, chopped	¼	cup	Dry white wine
1	tbsp	Olive oil	1	box	Triscuit Crackers, or substitute

Procedure

Immerse a cedar plank in water prior to starting this recipe to prevent burning of the wood.

Prepare your brie. This isn't difficult Dick so pay attention. Lay the brie down on the table and using a small paring knife, trace a circle around the top of the brie leaving about a ¼ inch lip on the outside edge. Just cut enough to pierce the rind. Next, trace out equal "pie slices" from within the circle, then gently peel away each slice to expose the top of the brie. Be careful to cut as little of the soft inner cheese as possible. Set aside.

Go outside and spark up the barbecue to medium heat so that it's ready when you are.

Now, finely chop the red pepper, shallot and garlic.

In a small frying pan, add olive oil and melt the butter on medium heat. Add the peppers and shallot, then sauté for five minutes or until mixture begins to soften. Next add garlic and Montreal Steak Spice, then cook for another two minutes.

Now add the wine, reduce heat and simmer for 10 more minutes until the wine is reduced and mixture is thick.

Spread mixture on top of the brie, keeping within the perimeter Dick, and place in the center of your cedar plank.

Turn off either the center our outside burner of your barbecue and place the cedar plank over the section of the barbecue that is NOT lit. Close the lid, and have a spray bottle with water handy to occasionally spray the cedar plank as the brie cooks.

Cook for approximately 20 minutes, or until Brie is soft in the center. Keep an eye on it Dick because if it cooks too long the outside edge will give way and your brie will look like a busted above ground swimming pool.

Remove from heat, and place in the center of a small serving plate. Serve with Triscuit or your favourite crackers.

Servings: 4

Dick's Difficulty Gauge: Easy

Preparation Time: 25 minutes
Cooking Time: 20 minutes
Total Time: 45 minutes

Dicks Tips

You can buy cedar planks dirt cheap at most grocery stores in the seafood department. They provide an amazing smoked flavor to dishes. If you don't have a barbeque, get one. You're a man for the love of God. In the meantime, you can cook the brie in the oven on a baking sheet instead at 375° F for 20 minutes, or until it appears soft and jiggly.

I'm The Man Hamburgers with Sautéed Onions

Every respectable Dick needs a good burger recipe and this is it. Super simple with high-speed taste.

2	lb	Lean ground beef	2 tbsp	Montreal Steak Spice
1	pkg	Lipton Onion Soup Mix	2 med	Cooking onions
2		Eggs, beaten	2 tbsp	Butter or margarine
½	cup	Italian style bread crumbs	2 tsp	Sugar
¼	cup	Barbecue sauce		

Procedure

Combine lean ground beef, soup mix, eggs, bread crumbs, your favorite barbecue sauce and some Montreal Steak Spice in a large bowl and mix well with hands.

Form into good sized patties and place in a baking dish or shallow container, then refrigerate for at least an hour.

Shortly before barbecuing, thinly slice your cooking onions and place in a small sauce pan with butter and sugar. Cook on medium heat, stirring occasionally until onions are soft and slightly opaque (clear looking). This will take about 20 minutes.

Meanwhile, spark up the barbee to medium heat and throw on your burgers. Be sure to flip them every five minutes or so for about twenty minutes.

Melt your favorite cheese on the patties just before removing from the barbecue and spoon some of the sautéed onions over top. Serve with some fresh buns (Kaisers are good) and your condiments of choice.

Servings: 8

Dick's Difficulty Gauge: Very easy

Preparation Time: 20 minutes
Cooking Time: 20 minutes
Total Time: 1 hour

Dicks Tips

The Dick Factor: Don't be a boring Dick with your cheese choice either. Why not try some Jalapeno Monterey Jack or Havarti slices instead? Go ahead, be crazy. And for you garlic lovers, opt for the Roasted Garlic Onion Soup Mix if you can find it. This serves well with Corn on a Bender and some Manly Macaroni Salad, not to mention it makes for great leftovers.

Love Slugs

Okay Dick, nothing says romance like Escargot. Historically used as an aphrodisiac, if you can't get your date warmed up with snails, then you might be on your own.

¼ cup Dick's Garlic Butter	12 large Escargots
1 tbsp Dried parsley	2 tbsp Butter
1 tsp Black pepper	¾ cup Dry white wine
1 dash Nutmeg	¼ cup Marble cheese, shredded
12 large Stuffing mushrooms	

Procedure

In a small dish, mix together Dick's Garlic Butter, parsley, pepper and nutmeg. Set aside until ready to use.

Preheat oven to 350° F.

Wash mushrooms and remove stems. (See tips Dick). Rinse and drain your snails.

In a medium sized sauce pan bring the butter and wine to a boil. Reduce heat then add the mushrooms and snails to the boiling wine and simmer for two minutes.

Remove from heat and strain mushrooms and snails with a strainer in the sink. Allow to cool until mushrooms can be handled. (About five minutes)

Lay each mushroom hollow side up, on a shallow baking dish. Place a snail into each mushroom cap. Then, using a teaspoon, spoon a scoop of Dick's Garlic Butter mixture into each mushroom, until level with the top of caps.

Sprinkle the top of the stuffed caps with the shredded cheese and place in oven, baking at 350° for 20 minutes, or until cheese is bubbling.

Remove from oven and serve on their own or with some thinly sliced garlic toasts. (A baguette would be a good choice here Dick.)

Servings: 2
Yield: 12

Dick's Difficulty Gauge: Easy

Oven Temperature: 350°F

Preparation Time: 25 minutes
Cooking Time: 20 minutes
Total Time: 45 minutes

Dicks Tips

Taking the stems off of mushrooms is a snap Dick but make sure your mushrooms are fresh. Gently snap off the stem and discard. Then, with a small spoon, lightly scrape the inside of the mushroom to remove all remnants of the stem, leaving a small hollow for your slugs. And remember that a 'dash' is a single shake of the spice container.

Nascar Nachos

Having the guys over for the big race? Well Dick you gotta feed them, and this hits the Winner's Circle with most. So heat up the oven, chill the beer and warm up the big screen.

1	lb	Lean ground beef	1	pkg	Tex Mex shredded cheese
1	pkg	Taco seasoning mix	1	cup	Green onions, chopped
1	cup	Water	1	cup	Tomatoes, chopped
1	cup	Chunky Salsa	1	cup	Pickled jalapeño peppers, sliced
1	bag	Nacho Chips			

Procedure

In a medium sized skillet (fry pan), brown the ground beef on medium high heat. Drain any excess fat.

Add the water, taco seasoning mix and salsa to the pan, and simmer on low heat until the mixture is thick (about 20 minutes).

In the meantime, preheat your oven to 350° F. If you don't have a baking dish that you can serve the nachos right out of, line a shallow pan or cookie sheet with tinfoil so that they can be easily lifted out onto a serving platter. This also makes for an easier clean up as melted cheese is a pain in the ass to clean.

Arrange a layer of nacho chips on the bottom of your baking dish. Spoon your hamburger mixture over layer and then top with some shredded cheese. Sprinkle with some green onion, tomato and jalapeño peppers, then repeat process with another layer of nachos. Depending on the size of your baking dish, you should get between three and four layers.

Bake nachos in the oven for approximately 15 minutes or until cheese is melted and nachos are slightly browned.

Serve immediately to all your pals with some sour cream, salsa and guacamole for dipping. Enjoy the race.

Servings: 6

Dick's Difficulty Gauge: Easy

Oven Temperature: 350°F

Preparation Time: 40 minutes
Cooking Time: 15 minutes
Total Time:

Dicks Tips

The Dick Factor: Substitute the ground beef mixture with three cups of left over Chili on a Bender for a different twist. For a healthier version, skip the ground beef all together and throw on three cups of diced cooked chicken.

Pigs and Popper's

This is a great appetizer Dick, but make sure your guests like it hot.

12	Jalapeño peppers	1 cup	Sharp cheddar cheese, grated
8oz	Cream cheese, room temperature	12 slices	Bacon, cut in half

Procedure

Preheat the oven to 450° F.

Cut the stem off of your peppers and then cut them in half lengthwise. Rinse with water to ensure all the seeds are removed. (These seeds are crazy hot and will burn your mouth if left in).

Spoon cream cheese into each pepper and then cover with the grated cheddar.

Wrap each pepper with a strip of bacon, being sure to cover the cream cheese filling as much as possible.

Place the poppers on a baking sheet sprayed with non-stick cooking spray and bake for 15 minutes or until bacon is fully cooked.

Remove from oven and allow to cool for about five minutes before serving. Serve on their own or with some ranch dressing on the side as a dipping sauce.

Servings: 4
Yield: 12

Dick's Difficulty Gauge: Very easy

Oven Temperature: 450°F

Preparation Time: 10 minutes
Cooking Time: 15 minutes
Inactive Time: 5 minutes
Total Time: 30 minutes

Dicks Tips

You may want to practice safe cooking and throw on some rubber gloves here Dick. If you choose not to, be very careful with your hands during and after cooking. Any touching of your eyes or other 'sensitive parts' could prove a tad bit uncomfortable.

Poker Pizza Dip

As far as dips go, this one is manly enough to serve to your buddies. Keep these simple ingredients on hand to whip up a quick appetizer for poker night...everyone will ante up!

1 pkg	Cream cheese - room temperature	½ cup	Pepperoni slices
2 tbsp	Italian spices		Pita bread
2 7.5oz	Pizza sauce cans		Garlic olive oil
4 cups	Grated mozzarella cheese		

Procedure

Preheat oven to 375° F.

Mix the cream cheese with the Italian spices and spread over the bottom of a 9 x 11 inch pan.

Spread out one of the cans of pizza sauce, and top with two cups of the mozzarella cheese.

Next spread the second can of pizza sauce out, followed by the remaining cheese.

Spread the pepperoni over the final layer and bake in the oven for 40 - 45 minutes, or until the top layer of cheese is bubbling.

Meanwhile brush the pita bread with some garlic flavored olive oil and then cut into bite sized triangles. Arrange on a cookie sheet.

When you remove the dip from the oven, place the pita wedges in and bake for ten minutes or until slightly browned.

Serve the pita wedges with the dip.

Servings: 6

Dick's Difficulty Gauge: Easy

Oven Temperature: 375°F

Preparation Time: 10 minutes
Cooking Time: 45 minutes
Total Time: 55 minutes

Dicks Tips

The Dick Factor: Throw some of your favorite veggie toppings on the dip prior to baking. You can also have a variety of 'dippers' such as nacho chips and bread sticks in addition to the pita wedges.

Real Men Do Cry French Onion Soup

Let this soup help you connect with your feminine side Dick. Its rich broth and slow cooked onions are perfect for a crisp autumn day. It will warm your belly and your soul.

2 tbsp	Olive oil	1 tsp	Herbes de Provence seasoning
½ cup	Butter		
5 large	Spanish onion, thinly sliced	1 tsp	Worcestershire sauce
		4	Bay leaves
2 tsp	Sugar	2 cups	Dick's Garlic Croutons (or alternatively slices of toasted baguette)
5 cups	Beef Broth		
1 cup	White wine		
½ cup	Cognac	2 cups	Shredded Gruyere cheese

Procedure

In a large sauce pan melt the olive oil and butter on medium high heat. Add the onions and sugar and cook for about 10 minutes, stirring frequently. The onions should start turning brown on the edges.

Now reduce the heat to the lowest setting and continue to cook for another 30 minutes.

Meanwhile, turn your crock-pot onto low. Add the beef broth, wine, cognac, Herbes de Provence, Worcestershire and bay leaves to the crock-pot,

Take your onions and add them to the crock-pot. Cover and cook slowly for about 5 hours.

When you're ready to serve, turn the broiler in the oven on high and grab your French onion soup bowls. Ladle each bowl to about ¾ full, throw in a handful of Dick's Garlic Croutons, and top with the shredded Gruyere cheese.

Arrange the French onion soup bowls on a cookie sheet and broil in the oven for 3 - 4 minutes or until your cheese is bubbly and starting to brown.

Remove from oven and carefully rest on a small plate lined with a napkin to keep the bowls from sliding.

Servings: 6

Dick's Difficulty Gauge: Moderately difficult

Preparation Time: 45 minutes
Cooking Time: 5 minutes
Inactive Time: 5 hours
Total Time: 5 hours and 50 minutes

Dicks Tips

If your eyes are sensitive to fresh cut onions Dick, try wearing your sunglasses or better yet some swimming goggles when you cut them up. Ya, you'll look goofy but you won't shed a tear.

The Dick Factor: Keep about a ¼ cup of crispy fried onions and sprinkle some on top of the melted cheese before serving.

Red Hot Red Pepper Soup

A bit of a pain in the ass to make, but well worth the effort!

5	Red bell peppers	¼ cup	Chopped fresh dill
2 tbsp	Butter	1 cup	Table cream (18%)
1 med	Cooking onions, chopped fine	3 dashes	Cayenne pepper
2 cups	Chicken broth	1 tsp	Paprika
1 cup	Dry white wine		Salt and pepper to taste
1 sprig	Fresh rosemary, stem off		

Procedure

Preheat oven to 400° F. Cut the tops off of the peppers, and core and seed them. Place them skin side up on a shallow baking dish and bake in the oven for approximately 30 minutes, or until skins become soft and bubble up. Don't worry if the skins start to darken.

Meanwhile, melt butter in a large soup pot and sauté onion on medium heat for ten minutes or until soft.

Add chicken soup broth, wine, rosemary and dill to soup pot, boiling softly on medium heat for twenty minutes.

When peppers are done, remove from baking dish and immerse briefly (30 seconds) in cold water to help loosen the skins. Remove from water, peel away skins and toss 'em. Put peeled peppers into soup pot and simmer for another five minutes.

Carefully pour soup mixture into a blender or food processor and blend until smooth or desired consistency is reached. Return to soup pot and stir in cream, cayenne, paprika, salt and pepper. Cook on medium low heat for at least 20 minutes and then simmer on low until ready to serve.

Servings: 4

Dick's Difficulty Gauge: Moderately difficult

Oven Temperature: 400°F

Preparation Time: 35 minutes
Cooking Time: 1 hour

Total Time: 1 hour and 35 minutes

Dicks Tips

The red peppers could also be roasted on the barbecue in advance instead of in the oven. If making this soup as an appetizer for a meal, prepare ahead of time and reheat when ready to serve or simply leave simmering on low heat.

The Dick Factor: If you want to be a fancy Dick cut a sprig of rosemary off and use as a garnish to float on top of the soup.

Reservoir Dogs Casserole

A spicy casserole great for the game or a manly flick. Be sure to have a reservoir of cold beer on hand to wash this down.

1 tbsp	Butter	¼ cup	Ketchup
½ cup	Chopped Spanish onions	½ tsp	Cayenne pepper
¾ cup	Yellow peppers, chopped	2½ cups	Biscuit baking mix
1 lb	Turkey or chicken wieners, cut into 1 inch pieces	1 cup	Cheddar cheese, grated
		¾ cup	Milk
1 16oz can	Baked beans		
½ cup	Sweet chili sauce		

Procedure

In a large skillet, melt butter on medium heat and sauté onions and peppers for ten minutes.

Stir in your wieners, beans, chili sauce, ketchup and cayenne pepper. Reduce heat and simmer for five minutes.

Remove mixture from heat and pour into a large casserole dish.

Preheat the oven to 350° F.

In a large bowl, combine the remaining ingredients to make the biscuit topping. Carefully spoon the topping over the meat mixture.

Bake uncovered in the oven for 25 to 30 minutes, or until biscuit topping is golden brown.

Servings: 6

Dick's Difficulty Gauge: Easy

Oven Temperature: 350°F

Preparation Time: 20 minutes
Cooking Time: 30 minutes
Total Time: 50 minutes

Dicks Tips

You can use regular wieners here Dick, but the turkey or chicken wieners will reduce the fat content with no change in taste.

She's Perfect Pesto Portabellas

This is a pretty simple, yet showy appetizer that's sure to impress your guests. Four ingredients and ten minutes on the grill, and once more you've outdone yourself.

4 lg	Portabella mushrooms, stemmed & washed	4 tbsp	Basil Pesto
2 tbsp	Olive oil	4 tbsp	Goat cheese

Procedure

Wash and stem your mushrooms, then pat dry with a paper towel. On the top (smooth side) brush each mushroom lightly with the olive oil.

Flip over and spoon one tablespoon of pesto onto each underbelly of the mushroom, and spread evenly.

Top the pesto with a tablespoon of goat cheese in the center of each mushroom.

Grill on the barbecue over medium heat (oiled side down Dick) for approximately ten minutes or until mushrooms appear moist and softened. Serve warm.

Servings: 4
Yield: 4

Dick's Difficulty Gauge: Very easy

Preparation Time: 5 minutes
Cooking Time: 10 minutes
Total Time: 15 minutes

Dicks Tips

This appetizer should serve one mushroom per guest depending on size. When choosing your portabella mushrooms, try to get fresh ones that are about 5 inches (12 cm) in diameter. There is no need to remove the 'fins' from the underbelly, just rinse well before preparing.

As for the pesto, you can find jars of this in the same aisle as you would purchase your pasta sauces. It's a versatile Dick Staple and always good to have handy.

Hot Mama Melts

Okay, so maybe not the healthiest choice, but holy man are these good. Serve them up to your buddies next time they're over... just keep the defibrillator charged.

1 cup	Butter, softened	
¼ cup	Green onions, finely chopped	
1 4oz can	Diced jalapeño peppers	
1 cup	Monterey Jack cheese, grated	

¼ cup	Mayonnaise
½ tsp	Garlic powder
1	French baguette

Procedure

Preheat oven to 400° F.

In a bowl, combine the butter, onion, peppers, cheese, mayo, and garlic powder.

Slice the baguette into ¼ inch thick slices and spread the mixture over top of each slice.

Bake on a cookie sheet for 10 minutes or until cheese starts to bubble and brown.

Servings: 4
Yield: 12

Dick's Difficulty Gauge: Very easy

Oven Temperature: 400°F

Preparation Time: 10 minutes
Cooking Time: 10 minutes
Total Time:

Dicks Tips

Baguettes usually don't keep fresh for too long Dick, so try to pick the loaf up that day or at most the day before. Also, I'll stress again not to use Miracle Whip here. Stick to the real thing my friend.

Single and Sexy Caesar Salad

So sexy you won't care about the garlic breath Dick. Use this as an appetizer or a side dish with any meat. Hell, use it as a main course with some chicken thrown on top. It will truly be the best Caesar salad you've ever had.

6 cups	Romaine lettuce, washed, dried and cut into bite sized pieces	¼ cup	Dick Likes It Creamy Caesar Salad Dressing
1 cup	Dicks croutons	1 tsp	Dried dill
7	Bacon slices, cooked and chopped		Freshly ground black pepper to taste

Procedure

Wash, dry and chop romaine. If you have a salad spinner to remove the excess water, use it. They rock. If not wash the romaine leaves, pat dry with a paper towel, then chop.

Microwave bacon slices for 8 minutes at 70% power, covered with a paper towel. Chop.

Combine all ingredients in a large bowl. Toss salad to coat. Add more or less dressing according to taste.

Servings: 4

Dick's Difficulty Gauge: Very easy

Preparation Time: 15 minutes
Cooking Time:
Total Time:

Dicks Tips

You can prepare your romaine, bacon and croutons ahead of time and then keep cold in the fridge until ready to serve. Mix just before serving for a crisp, cold, rocking salad.

Sloppy Dicks

Long night out leaving you feeling like a soup sandwich? Well here's a real soup sandwich to help put you back together. A lighter version of Sloppy Joes this is sure to stick to your ribs and have you cleaning your plate. (Just don't lick the plate Dick...not cool.)

3 tbsp	Butter	
½ cup	Green peppers, chopped	
½ cup	Red onions, chopped	
1 cup	Mushrooms, sliced or chopped	
1 lb	Ground turkey	
2 10oz	Cans condensed cream of mushroom soup	
½ cup	White wine	
1 tbsp	Montreal Steak Spice	
1 tsp	Garlic Powder	
1 tsp	Ground black pepper	
4 dashes	Worcestershire sauce	
4 dashes	Tabasco or hot sauce	
	Fresh Kaiser rolls	

Procedure

In a large frying pan on medium heat, melt butter and add peppers, onions and mushrooms. Sauté for approximately 15 minutes, or until vegetables soften.

Next add the ground turkey to the pan, cooking through until browned and no longer pink, about 10 minutes.

In a separate bowl, whisk together soup and wine until smooth. Reduce heat to medium low and gradually stir in soup mixture to meat and vegetables.

Add the remaining spices. When mixture begins to boil, reduce heat to low and simmer for 15 minutes, stirring occasionally. Add additional seasons to suit taste.

Spoon mixture over fresh cut Kaiser Rolls and serve.

Servings: 4

Dick's Difficulty Gauge: Easy

Preparation Time: 15 minutes
Cooking Time: 40 minutes
Total Time: 55 minutes

Dicks Tips

You can substitute milk for the wine here. Just be careful not to thin the mixture out too much. You don't want it runny Dick. Instead strive for a thicker consistency for your soup sandwich. Feel free to experiment with your spices here as well. It's your recipe, anything goes!

Smokin' Gouda Dip

Whether you make this for the boys or your smoking hot date, this artichoke dip with a twist will have them licking their fingers. Watch out for the double dipper.

- 1 pkg Cream cheese - room temperature
- 1 cup Mayonnaise
- ½ cup Parmesan cheese
- 1 cup Smoked Gouda Cheese, grated
- 1 tbsp Dijon mustard
- 2 Garlic cloves, chopped or minced
- 1 tbsp Worcestershire sauce
- 1 can Artichoke hearts, drained and chopped (14oz)
- Crackers or pita chips

Procedure

Preheat your oven to 375° F, and lightly spray a medium sized baking dish with cooking spray.

Using an electric mixer, combine all ingredients except the artichokes in a bowl and beat until well blended.

Using a spoon or spatula, mix in the drained and chopped artichoke hearts.

Spoon mixture into the baking dish and bake for 20 minutes or until the mixture starts to bubble.

Serve with crackers or pita chips.

Servings: 6
Yield: About 4 cups

Dick's Difficulty Gauge: Easy

Oven Temperature: 375°F

Preparation Time: 10 minutes
Cooking Time: 20 minutes
Total Time: 30 minutes

Dicks Tips

The Dick Factor: This dip rocks Dick. It is perfectly fine on its own, but if you'd like to jazz it up a little, throw in a package of drained and chopped frozen spinach or a cup of chopped up crab meat. Leftovers are extremely unlikely.

Stalker Soup

A super simple cream of asparagus and celery soup recipe to enjoy with your date, or alone while she watches you through the window.

¼ cup	Butter or margarine	1½ lbs	Fresh asparagus
6	celery stalks, chopped	1 cup	Half and half cream
4	Shallots, finely chopped	½ tsp	Salt
4 cups	Chicken broth	½ tsp	White pepper

Procedure

In a medium sized sauce pan, melt butter over medium heat and sauté celery and shallots for five minutes or until soft.

In the same pot, add 2 cups of the broth and simmer for 20 minutes.

Add the asparagus and cook for an additional 10 minutes, or until tender.

Transfer soup mixture to a blender, and puree until smooth. (Careful Dick, it's hot.)

Add the remaining unused broth to the pan, stirring occasionally. Cook for 10 minutes longer or until heated.

Return the blended soup mixture to the pan, then add the cream, salt and pepper. Cook on medium low, stirring often for 10 to 15 minutes.

Serve hot.

Servings: 4
Yield: 6 cups

Dick's Difficulty Gauge: Moderately difficult

Preparation Time: 10 minutes
Cooking Time: 1 hour
Total Time: 1 hour and 10 minutes

Dicks Tips

Keep an eye on anything you cook with milk or cream in it, as it will burn to the bottom of the pan if not stirred enough.

The Dick Factor: Take a couple of your reserved asparagus spears and put two in each bowl as a garnish right before serving.

The Super Bowl Cheese Fondue

Okay Dick...granted you may never host a fondue party. A Super Bowl party however? Now we're talking. This one you can pull off and you don't even need a pot. And remember Dick, what happens at football, stays at football.

2	loaf	Round Bread (8 - 10 inches)	½ cup		Chopped green onions
2	cups	Sharp cheddar cheese, shredded	1	tbsp	Herbs de Provence
2	pkg	Cream Cheese, softened	1	tbsp	Worcestershire sauce
1½	cups	Sour cream	1	tsp	Frank's Hot Sauce
1	cup	Ham, diced and cooked	1	tbsp	Garlic olive oil

Procedure

Preheat your oven to 350° F.

Slice a thin portion off the top of one of the bread rounds, being sure the hole is smaller than the diameter of the bread. Hollow the remainder of the bread out, leaving the crust of the bread bowl intact. Set the removed bread and cap aside.

In a large bowl combine shredded cheddar, cream cheese, sour cream, ham, onion, Herbs de Provence, Worcestershire, hot sauce and mix until well blended. You may want to use an electric mixer for this if you have one available.

Spoon mixture into the hollowed loaf until full, and then replace the cap of the bread.

Wrap the entire loaf in about five layers of tin foil. Place on a cookie sheet on the center rack of the oven and bake at 350° F for 1 hour 15 minutes.

While your bread bowl is baking, tear up the bread from the first round into bite sized pieces. Chop or tear the second round into bit sized pieces as well. Arrange the bread on a large cookie sheet.

Brush the bread with the garlic flavored olive oil, or garlic butter. Once you remove the bread bowl from the oven, place the bread pieces in and bake for approximately 10 minutes, or until lightly browned.

Carefully unwrap your bread bowl and place on a serving plate. Throw the toasted bread crumbs around it or in a separate serving bowl, remove the cap and enjoy.

Servings: 8

Dick's Difficulty Gauge: Easy

Oven Temperature: 350°F

Preparation Time: 30 minutes
Cooking Time: 1 hour and 30 minutes
Total Time: 2 hours

Dicks Tips

You can find a Bread Pot or Bread Round at pretty much any grocery store bakery section. Try the sour dough, pumpernickel or one of both. The Herbs de Provence is located in the spices section…just scan alphabetically. It's a great spice to keep on hand for other recipes as well.

The Dick Factor: While the bread is good for dipping in this recipe fresh cut veggies are great too. Put out some chopped peppers, mushrooms, broccoli, cauliflower and celery for the health wary snacker's. Also, if you can find it, a football shaped bread bowl would be perfect here.

Wingman

Every guy needs a professional wingman and every guy needs a kick-ass wing recipe. No deep fryer required for these babies Dick, but they'll taste like they're restaurant quality.

8 cups	Water	1 tbsp	Garlic powder
4 cups	Chicken broth	½ tsp	Cayenne pepper
1 cup	Italian Style seasoned breadcrumbs	½ cup	Melted butter
1 cup	Grated Parmesan cheese	4 lbs	Chicken wings
¼ cup	Whole wheat flour		Sea salt and cracked black pepper

Procedure

Bring your water and chicken broth to a full boil over high heat. Add your wings and cook for 15 minutes before removing from pot and allowing to slightly cool.

Preheat oven to 425° F. Line a cookie sheet with tin foil and spray generously with non-stick cooking spray.

In a plastic bowl with a tight fitting lid, combine bread crumbs, parmesan cheese, whole wheat flour, garlic powder and cayenne. Mix thoroughly to fully combine the seasoning.

Using a pastry brush coat the chicken wings with a thin layer of the melted butter.

Place 3 - 5 wings at a time (depending on size of your bowl) into the seasoning mixture. Seal the container and toss the wings to coat with the seasoning.

Arrange wings on the cookie sheet and season with sea salt and cracked pepper according to your own taste.

Bake in the pre-heated oven for 30 minutes or until the skin appears crisp and golden.

Serve with some ranch or blue cheese dressing for a dip.

Servings: 4
Yield: 4 lbs

Dick's Difficulty Gauge: Easy

Oven Temperature: 425°F

Preparation Time: 30 minutes
Cooking Time: 30 minutes
Total Time: 1 hour

Dicks Tips

What you're doing here Dick is something called par boiling. This is done to partially cook something before finishing the process through another means - enter the oven. It gets rid of some of the fat as well and will give you a juicier wing with that crispy coating.

GOING, GOING, GONE…

*"Don't let love interfere with your appetite.
It never does with mine."*
~ Anthony Trollope

Banger and Dash

A simple, somewhat healthier version of Bangers and Mash...sure to give you enough energy to get out of Dodge.

6	lg	Baking potatoes, peeled and quartered	1	tbsp	Butter
1	tbsp	Butter	1		Cooking onion, diced
¼	cup	Milk	1	pkg	Dry gravy mix
1	tsp	Paprika	1	cup	Water
1½	lbs	Turkey sausages, sliced into ½ inch pieces. (Or other low-fat sausages)	1	cap	Mrs. Dash Extra Spicy seasoning

Procedure

Preheat the oven to 350° F.

Place potatoes in a large pot with enough water to cover them. Cover and boil on high heat for about 20 minutes or until soft. Drain water and mash with butter, milk and paprika until smooth. Cover and set aside to keep warm.

In a large frying pan over medium heat, fry sausage pieces for 15 minutes or until cooked through. Remove from pan and set aside.

Using the same pan, melt one tablespoon of butter and add onions. Sauté for 10 minutes or until onions begin to soften.

Add the remaining ingredients to the pan bringing to a boil. Reduce to simmer and stir continuously to ensure your gravy is lump-free and thick. Remove from heat.

Pour enough of the gravy mix into a casserole dish, to just cover the bottom. Add the cooked sausage over the gravy, then pour remaining gravy over sausage. Top with mashed potatoes.

Bake uncovered for 20 minutes, or until potatoes are lightly browned.

Servings: 6

Dick's Difficulty Gauge: Easy

Oven Temperature: 350°F

Preparation Time: 15 minutes
Cooking Time: 1 hour and 30 minutes
Total Time: 1 hour and 45 minutes

Dicks Tips

If you want a quick short-cut Dick, make yourself a batch of instant potatoes instead of mashed from scratch. The butter and herb or garlic versions would be good here. As for the sausage, Bob's your uncle, but the lower fat versions will be better for your ticker and your waistline.

Bite Me Sheppard's Pie

So the 'not-so-future Mrs. Dick' hates spicy food? Well nothing says bite me like a serving of spicy Sheppard's Pie. A hot twist on an old classic, for a final adios.

8 med	Potatoes, peeled and diced (about 2 lbs)	1	lb	Lean ground beef
¼ cup	Butter	1	35g pkg	Taco seasoning mix
¼ cup	Milk	1½ cups		Frozen kernel corn
1 tbsp	Butter	1	cup	Shredded jalapeño Monterey Jack cheese
½ cup	Spanish onion, finely chopped			

Procedure

In a large pot full of water, bring potatoes to a boil and cook for 20 minutes or until soft. Drain potatoes, then mash with butter and milk until smooth. Set aside, covered to keep warm.

Preheat oven to 350° F.

In a large fry pan on medium heat, melt remaining butter and sauté onions until soft, for about ten minutes.

Add the ground beef and fry until browned, being sure to break up the ground beef as much as possible. Drain any excess fat.

Stir in taco seasoning mix and corn, cooking for five minutes on medium-low heat.

Spread a thin layer of the mashed potatoes over the bottom of a 2 quart casserole dish. Next, spread the ground beef mixture over top of potatoes. Sprinkle the shredded cheese over ground beef, and top with remaining mashed potatoes.

Bake uncovered for 30 to 40 minutes or until the mashed potatoes form a light brown crust.

Servings: 6

Dick's Difficulty Gauge: Easy

Oven Temperature: 350°F

Preparation Time: 1 hour
Cooking Time: 40 minutes
Total Time: 1 hour and 40 minutes

Dicks Tips

Looking for a shortcut Dick? Buy yourself a box of instant mashed potatoes and cook according to package directions to substitute for the mashed potatoes from scratch. Spreading milk over the top of the mashed potatoes will help to form a nice brown crust.

For a not-so-spicy version, substitute the jalapeno Monterey jack cheese for shredded marble or cheddar.

The Dick Factor: Brushing the potato topping about 15 minutes before its done will brown the top of the potatoes nicely.

Blackened Sole

Well soul mates you're not, but there's always next time. Meanwhile, feel sorry for yourself over blackened sole and get ready for the next Mrs. Right. (Or Mrs. Right-Now...whatever.)

½ cup	Complete Buttermilk Pancake Mix	1 tsp	Mesquite Seasoning
1 tbsp	Paprika	1 tsp	Herbes de Provence
1 tbsp	Coarse Salt	3 tbsp	Olive oil
1 tsp	Onion powder	½ cup	Butter, melted
1 tsp	Garlic powder	4 fillets	Sole, fresh if possible

Procedure

Mix all the dry ingredients until thoroughly combined.

Using a large frying pan or cast iron skillet, heat olive oil until hot on medium high heat.

Brush the fish with the melted butter until it is coated on both sides. Coat the fish with the dry spice mixture on both sides.

Lay the fish into the frying pan. Fry for 3 minutes then carefully flip over and fry for another 3 minutes.

Remove from pan and place in a serving platter lined with paper-towel to soak up excess oil. Keep warm until ready to serve.

Servings: 4

Dick's Difficulty Gauge: Easy

Preparation Time: 5 minutes
Cooking Time: 6 minutes
Total Time: 11 minutes

Dicks Tips

Pretty much any flaky white fish will do here Dick, but Sole is a good choice. If you can't get fresh, don't sweat it, frozen is just as good. Don't compromise with smelly fish. You'll be sorry.

Cold Shoulder, Hot Catfish

Light and spicy Dick, this is a fast and easy fish dish. The cage will make you look like a barbecue guru and catfish is a nice healthy dinner.

4 fillets	Catfish, fresh		1 tsp	White pepper
1 tbsp	Olive oil		1 tsp	Black pepper freshly ground
1 tbsp	Cajun seasoning		¼ tsp	Cayenne pepper
2 tsp	Paprika			Non-stick cooking spray
1 tsp	Lemon pepper seasoning		2 med	Lemons

Procedure

Heat the barbecue to medium high.

Wash your fillet's with cold water and pat dry with a paper towel.

Rub a small amount of olive oil onto the fillets - just enough to coat.

Combine all of the dry spices in a shallow dish making sure they're well blended.

Season both sides of the catfish with the spice mixture by sprinkling on with your fingers and rubbing the fish to coat.

Using a barbecue cage, spray with non-stick cooking spray. Arrange the fish equal distances apart and close cage as close to fish as possible.

Cook over grill for five to seven minutes. Flip cage and cook for an additional five minutes, or until fish is white and flaky.

Grill your lemon halves face down for the last five minutes of barbecuing.

Open cage and release. Throw the grilled lemons beside the fish face up for effect and flavour.

Servings: 4

Dick's Difficulty Gauge: Very easy

Preparation Time: 5 minutes
Cooking Time: 15 minutes
Total Time: 20 minutes

Dicks Tips

Okay, so what exactly is a barbecue cage? You'll find it in cooking stores or most places that sell barbecue accessories and it's a great tool for Dick's kitchen.

A Swing and a Miss Chipotle Chicken

Struck out on Mrs. Right yet again Dick? The chipotle peppers in this dish will burn away any last memory of what's-her-name.

2	tbsp	Olive oil	¼	cup	Dry white wine
1	tbsp	Butter	1		Chipotle pepper
4		Boneless skinless chicken breasts	1	cube	Chicken bouillon
¾	cup	Half and half cream	1	clove	Garlic, minced
1	cup	Light sour cream			Salt and pepper to taste

Procedure

In a large skillet or electric frying pan, heat olive oil and butter over medium heat. Pan fry the chicken breasts until lightly browned on both sides, about 10 minutes.

Meanwhile, using a blender or food processor, puree the remaining ingredients until smooth.

Once chicken is browned, pour the sauce over the chicken and heat until it begins to lightly boil. Reduce heat to medium low, and simmer chicken in sauce for an additional 15 minutes, turning chicken occasionally to coat.

Remove from pan and serve with a little bit of the sauce poured over chicken.

Servings: 4

Dick's Difficulty Gauge: Easy

Preparation Time: 5 minutes
Cooking Time: 30 minutes
Total Time: 35 minutes

Dicks Tips

What the hell is a Chipotle pepper and where do you find it? It's a smoke dried jalapeno chili pepper, found in the Mexican food section of the grocery store, usually in a small can. These babies are super-hot, but super flavorful and a little goes a long way. If you like a little zing, stick to one pepper. If you want to man-up Dick, try two or three but have a cold drink handy.

Feeling Smothered Pasta

Feeling smothered? Pull the pin with this great chicken pasta dish that's loaded with flavour. This one's good for you too Dick - unlike your soon-to-be-excused dinner guest.

½ cup	Olive oil	1 lg	Green Pepper - chopped
4	Garlic cloves, chopped or minced	2 lg	Boneless skinless chicken breasts, chopped into bite sized pieces
1 tbsp	Pesto		
1 tsp	Salt and pepper to taste	1 can	Diced tomatoes - drained
1 pkg	Whole wheat spaghetti - cooked as per package directions.	½ cup	Green olives with pimento, chopped
1 tbsp	Butter	1 tbsp	Red pepper flakes
1 tbsp	Olive oil		
½ lg	Spanish Onion - chopped		

Procedure

In a small bowl combine olive oil, garlic, pesto, salt and pepper. Allow to sit for a half hour or more for the flavours to blend, stirring occasionally.

In a large pot, boil water and cook pasta following the directions on the box. Once cooked, drain, rinse and cover to keep warm.

In a large frying pan, heat olive oil and butter on medium heat. Once butter has melted sauté onions for 2 - 3 minutes or until they just begin to soften.

Add the green peppers and chicken, and continue to cook until chicken is cooked through or about 10 minutes.

Next add the diced tomatoes, green olives and red pepper flakes, stirring to heat throughout. Simmer on low for five more minutes.

Take your warm pasta and toss with the olive oil and pesto sauce, ensuring to evenly coat. (If you need to reheat your pasta Dick just place it in a colander and strain with hot water to warm it back up before tossing with the olive oil.)

Spoon your pasta onto a plate and then top with the chicken and tomato mixture from the pan. Serve immediately.

Servings: 4

Dick's Difficulty Gauge: Easy

Preparation Time: 15 minutes
Cooking Time: 25 minutes
Inactive Time: 30 minutes
Total Time: 1 hour and 10 minutes

Dicks Tips

This is a good time to whip up some Dick's Bread n' Butter garlic bread to serve with this pasta dish.

It's Not Me, It's You Meatloaf

While this dish is a guarantee, don't use the title as the opener. Repeat after me Dick: It's not you, it's me, and I'm sorry...There you go.

2	lbs	Lean ground beef	1	sm	Jalapeno pepper seeded and finely chopped (see Tips Dick)
2	lg	Eggs, beaten	½	cup	Italian Style seasoned breadcrumbs
½	cup	Chili Pepper sauce			
1	cup	Mushrooms, chopped	1	pkg	Lipton's Onion Roasted Garlic soup mix
½	cup	Red peppers, chopped			
			2		Garlic cloves, crushed
			¼	cup	Chili Pepper sauce

Procedure

Preheat oven to 350° F.

Mix all ingredients together in a bowl, being sure to thoroughly combine. This is best done old school Dick, using your hands,

Spray a 9' x 5' loaf pan and place the hamburger in, shaping to fill the pan. Bake for 1 hour and 20 minutes.

Remove from oven and spread additional chili sauce over top of meatloaf, ensuring to cover the top of the loaf. Place back in oven and broil on low for 10 minutes. Keep an eye on this Dick to make sure it doesn't start to burn.

Remove from oven and drain off any excess fat by tilting the corner of the pan over the sink or a drip can. Let stand for ten minutes and then slice and serve!

Servings: 4

Dick's Difficulty Gauge: Easy

Oven Temperature: 350°F

Preparation Time: 20 minutes
Cooking Time: 1 hour and 40 minutes
Total Time: 2 hours

Dicks Tips

I'm going to do you a big fave here Dick and caution you about the perils of cutting and seeding jalapeno peppers. Wash your hands. And when you're done that, wash your hands again. Do not put your hands or fingers anywhere that may cause you...discomfort, prior to washing your hands. You've been warned.

Jerk-Off Chicken

If jerk isn't the worst thing you've been called this week try a stay-cation in the islands with this Jamaican inspired recipe. And remember Dick...you're not a jerk, you're just a guy.

- 2 tbsp Brown sugar
- 2 tbsp Garlic powder
- 1 tbsp Onion powder
- 1 tbsp Salt
- 1 tsp Black pepper
- 1 tsp Nutmeg
- 1 tsp Allspice
- 1 tsp Ginger
- 1 tbsp Cayenne
- 1 tsp Cinnamon
- ¼ cup Olive oil
- 6 Chicken legs (thigh and drumstick attached with skin on)
- 1 Lime cut in half
- ¼ cup Cilantro, chopped

Procedure

Throw all of the spices into a small bowl Dick - using an airtight container with a lid will keep the leftover spice mixture for next time.

Rinse your chicken legs with water and pat dry with a paper towel.

Rub a thin layer of olive oil all over the legs.

Rub your spice mixture all over the legs, making sure that you evenly coat them.

Spark up the barbecue to medium heat and roast these babies nice and slow so we don't burn the seasoning. This should take about 25 - 30 minutes.

About a minute before you remove the legs from the barbecue, squeeze your lime juice all over the legs.

Place the legs on a serving tray and sprinkle with your chopped cilantro. No problem Mon.

Servings: 6

Dick's Difficulty Gauge: Easy

Preparation Time: 15 minutes
Cooking Time: 30 minutes
Total Time: 45 minutes

Dicks Tips

You want to stick to the grill for this one Dick but you can throw this in the oven if you're stuck at about 375° F for an hour or so. If you're a big fan of the rub, you can always double up the recipe, store in an airtight container and it will keep for the next time you want to escape jerk status.

Let Her Down Easy Eggplant Parmesan

If you're going to be a heart breaker balance it off with some food that's good for the ticker as well. The eggplant and tomato sauce will be chock-full of antioxidants and a nice glass of red wine will boost your health and your mood.

2 lg	Eggplants, sliced into rounds no thicker than ½ inch	1½ cups	Italian seasoned bread crumbs
1 tbsp	Sea salt	½ cup	Grated Parmesan cheese
3 cups	Six Month Mari-Me-Nara Sauce or alternate spaghetti sauce	1 lb	Mozzarella cheese shredded
½ cup	Whole wheat flour	½ cup	Grated Parmesan cheese
4 lg	Eggs, lightly beaten	1 tsp	Herbes de Provence seasoning

Procedure

Wash and slice your eggplants. Lightly salt the rounds and lay out on a paper towel for 1 - 2 hours.

Heat up your Six Month Mari-Me-Nara sauce in a medium sauce pan, and simmer to keep warm.

Preheat oven to 400° F and spray two baking sheets with non-stick cooking spray.

Place your flour in a separate shallow dish.

Beat your egg in small bowl.

Combine your bread crumbs and a half cup of parmesan cheese in a shallow dish.

Now get your work station ready Dick and place the flour, egg and bread crumb bowls beside each other in that order.

Pat your eggplant slices with a paper towel to absorb any excess moisture.

Dip your eggplant rounds one at a time into the flour, then egg, then bread crumb mixture.

Spread out on the baking sheet and bake for 20 minutes, flipping rounds over half way through. They should be lightly browned when done.

Remove from oven and allow to cool off until you can easily handle them. Reduce oven temperature to 350° F.

Spray a 9" x 13" baking dish with non-stick cooking spray then spread 1 cup of your sauce in the bottom of the baking dish.

Place your eggplants along the bottom of the baking dish in a single layer. Cover this with half of the remaining sauce then sprinkle with half the mozzarella and half the parmesan cheese. Repeat this step for the second layer.

Sprinkle the top layer of cheese with your Herbes de Provence and bake at 350° F for 25 - 30 minutes or until the top is bubbly and a little bit browned.

Servings: 8

Dick's Difficulty Gauge: Moderately difficult

Oven Temperature: 350°F

Preparation Time: 1 hour
Cooking Time: 30 minutes
Inactive Time: 2 hours
Total Time: 3 hours and 30 minutes

Dicks Tips

If you're wondering why the hell you have to leave your eggplants out for two hours with some salt on them, it's so you can draw some of the moisture out Dick. Otherwise your eggplant may turn out soggy and we don't want that. You don't need to peel these either.

If you need your meat Dick brown up some low-fat turkey sausage and throw it into your sauce. Let's try to keep this one on the healthy side.

One Crazy Taco

Try this for a Cinco de Mayo dinner Dick. A snappy alternative to your typical taco, this one calls for fish instead of hamburger and is served with some homemade sauce with some zing.

½	cup	Sour cream	1	cup	Red or Green Onion, chopped
½	cup	Mayonnaise	1	cup	Baby spinach leaves, chopped
1		Lime	2	cups	Cheddar cheese, grated
1	tsp	Herbes de Provence seasoning	5	fillets	Tilapia
¼	tsp	Chipotle pepper			Cajun seasoning
1	tbsp	Hot sauce			Sea salt and cracked black pepper
1	tbsp	Cilantro, chopped			
2	med	Tomatoes, chopped	2	tbsp	Olive oil
			8	lg	Tortilla shells

Procedure

- In a small bowl or dish, mix together sour cream and mayo. Cut your lime in half and squeeze the juice of each half into the sour cream and mayo, then mix in. Next add the Herbes de Provence, chipotle pepper, hot sauce and cilantro. Cover and refrigerate for an hour or more to allow the flavours to blend.
- Now, chop up your vegetables and place each in a small bowl for fixings for your tacos, along with your cheese. Once these are ready, set aside or throw them on the table.
- Season each side of your tilapia fillets with some Cajun seasoning and salt and pepper. Heat the olive oil in a large non-stick frying pan on medium-high heat. Pan-fry each fillet approximately five minutes per side, or until white and flaky. Remove from heat.
- Slice your fish into thin strips and pile on a plate.
- Stack your tortilla shells on a large plate and heat in the microwave for 30 seconds. Split the tortillas and re-stack them, then zap them for another 30 seconds in the microwave.

Place all the ingredients, including the sauce on the table and allow your guests to stuff their tacos as they so choose.

Throw some hot sauce on the table too for those of your guests that like a little more zing.

Servings: 6

Dick's Difficulty Gauge: Easy

Preparation Time: 1 hour
Cooking Time: 10 minutes
Total Time: 30 minutes

Dicks Tips

Okay Dick, I've called for Tilapia in this recipe, but catfish or any other white, flaky fish would cut the mustard as well.

Dick Factor: To really add some festive flare, serve your tacos with some margaritas and do it up Mexican style.

ShishkaDicks

These Kabob's are one of my most requested recipes Dick. What separates the wheat from the chaff here is the addition of bacon and Halloom cheese which knocks these out of the park.

3	lg	Boneless skinless chicken breasts cut into 1" cubes	1	lg	Spanish onion, chopped into large 1" pieces
1	bot	Greek Style Marinade	½	lb	Bacon, cut in half with each piece rolled up.
2	pkg	Halloom Cheese cut into 1" cubes (12 per package, so you should end up with 24 cubes)			Season Salt to taste Celery Salt to taste
3	lg	Red, green or yellow bell peppers, chopped into large 1" pieces	1	cup	Dick's Tzatziki Sauce (See Dick's Staples) or store bought tzatziki.
12	lg	Mushrooms, washed and whole			

Procedure

Combine your chicken cubes and marinade in a small dish and allow to sit refrigerated for an hour or more.

Chop and prepare your cheese, peppers and onion. Wash your mushrooms and pat dry.

Assemble all of your kabob ingredients together and using your 12" skewers begin threading all of your ingredients. I would suggest you start with a mushroom at the base then equally thread the rest. You should have at least two pieces of Halloom cheese, three pieces of chicken and two pieces of bacon per kabob. The rest will be peppers and onion.

Lightly sprinkle the kabob's with Season salt and Celery salt.

Heat the barbecue to medium-low for this one Dick. You'll need to grill the kabobs slow enough to cook the chicken without charring your vegetables or melting your cheese to the point it falls off.

Place the kabobs directly on the grill and flip every few minutes to cook evenly throughout. This should take about 30 - 40 minutes or until your chicken is thoroughly cooked.

Remove from heat and serve with Dick's Tzatziki Sauce for dipping.

Servings: 4
Yield: 12

Dick's Difficulty Gauge: Easy

Preparation Time: 45 minutes
Cooking Time: 30 minutes
Inactive Time: 1 hour
Total Time: 2 hours and 15 minutes

Dicks Tips

Halloom cheese is a semi-soft cheese that is designed for grilling as it will keep its shape and resist melting so long as you cook it slow enough and at a moderate heat. I guarantee you that your guests will be raving about it. It will be found in the specialty cheese section of the deli and will be wrapped in a folded cube. Unfold the cheese and cut each half into six equal pieces. Don't try to cut these too small or they'll fall right off the skewer Dick.

If you don't have time to whip up your own Dick's Tzatziki Sauce then you will find the store bought varieties with all of the other special dips and sauces also near the deli section of the grocery store Dick. This is a must for this recipe as it's great as a dip for your kabobs, or should I say ShishkaDicks.

Stick a Fork In It Porchetta Roast

When it's done, it's done Dick. This slow cooked pork roast will give you all day to figure out your next steps. Tomorrow is another day.

4 tbsp	Olive oil		2 tsp	Black pepper corns
6	Garlic cloves - coarsely chopped		1 tsp	Red pepper flakes
¼ cup	Fresh rosemary, stem off and chopped		5 lbs	Boneless pork shoulder, excess fat trimmed off
1 tbsp	Dried oregano		1 cup	Dry white wine
1 tbsp	Sea salt		½ cup	Chicken broth
1 tbsp	Dried fennel seeds			

Procedure

In a small food processor, puree olive oil, garlic, rosemary, oregano, salt, fennel seeds, peppercorns, and red pepper flakes to form a paste.

Rub mixture all over the pork shoulder and cover with saran wrap. Allow pork to marinate in the refrigerator overnight Dick. A good 24 hours if you can manage to plan ahead.

Remove the pork from the fridge the next day about 2 hours prior to cooking it and allow to warm.

Turn the crock-pot on to high setting.

In a large frying pan over medium heat, sear all sides of the pork. About two minutes a side Dick. Remove pork and place in the crock-pot,

Add your wine and chicken broth to the frying pan and bring to a low boil for five minutes, combining the remaining juices from the pan.

Now add the wine and broth to the crock-pot. Cover and cook for one hour on high. Reduce the crock-pot temperature to medium and cook for another 5 - hours.

Servings: 8

Dick's Difficulty Gauge: Moderately difficult

Preparation Time: 30 minutes
Cooking Time: 6 hours

Total Time: 6 hours and 30 minutes

Dicks Tips

Some Gold Digger Scalloped Potatoes would be a great side for this meat. Leftovers, if there are any, can be used for pulled pork sandwiches.

We're Better Off Friends Fettuccini

Making the transition to 'friends with benefits' can be tricky Dick. Lucky for you this dish isn't tricky at all. Now you just have to figure out how to broach the subject...

1	12oz pkg	Fettuccine noodles - cooked as per package directions	¼ tsp	White pepper
			3 tbsp	Cream cheese
			½ cup	Grated Parmesan cheese
½	cup	Butter	½ cup	Grated Romano cheese
1		Shallot, finely chopped	¼ cup	Fresh parsley, chopped
1½	cups	Heavy cream		
2	cloves	Garlic, minced		
¼	tsp	Salt		

Procedure

Cook your fettuccine in a large pot of boiling salted water, or according to package directions until desired consistency is reached. Drain pasta keeping about ¼ cup of the liquid.

In a medium sized sauce pan over medium-high heat, melt your butter and add shallots. Sauté for about five minutes or until they begin to soften. Watch your heat here Dick. If your butter starts to brown, turn it down.

Reduce heat to medium low and add your cream, garlic, salt and pepper. Bring sauce to a low simmer, ensuring it doesn't reach a full boil. Stir this often Dick and simmer for 5 - 10 minutes or until sauce thickens.

Now add the cream cheese, parmesan and Romano cheese. (If you opt for the Dick Factor this is when you would add your meat.) Stir for 2 -3 minutes until cheeses are melted and well blended with the sauce.

Now take your pasta and put it back into the pot it was cooked in. Cooking over medium-high heat add your sauce to the pot and stir to completely coat your pasta. If your sauce is too thick for your liking here Dick, just add some of the liquid I told you to keep from when you cooked the pasta until your desired consistency is reached.

You'll want to serve this immediately Dick because it cools fast. Spoon generous portions onto the plates and sprinkle the top with some chopped fresh parsley.

Now...where were we?

Servings: 4

Dick's Difficulty Gauge: Easy

Preparation Time: 15 minutes
Cooking Time: 20 minutes
Total Time: 35 minutes

Dicks Tips

If you can find it, some fresh pasta would be great here as opposed to the boxed versions.

Dick Factor: To really impress throw in 2 cups of cooked diced chicken breast or shrimp. Hell - throw them both in, and serve with Dick's Bread n' Butter.

Splitsville Pea Soup

Splitsville...population one. Nothing warms the soul like some hot soup with hot sausage. This should last you the week while you lick your wounds, and the bowl.

2 tbsp	Olive oil	8 cups	Chicken broth
4 tbsp	Butter	4 cups	Water
1 med	Cooking onion, chopped	1 tbsp	Parsley
2	Carrots, peeled and shredded	2 cups	Split peas, green or yellow
2	Celery stalks, chopped	1½ cups	Italian sausage, cooked and diced
2	Garlic cloves, crushed		Salt and pepper to taste

Procedure

In a large soup pot, melt butter and olive oil together on medium heat.

Add onion, carrots, celery and garlic then sauté until tender, about 10 minutes.

Increase heat to high and add chicken broth, water and parsley.

Using a strainer, rinse peas in cold water and then add to soup pot, bringing to a boil. Boil on high for 10 minutes then reduce heat to low.

Add sausage and salt and pepper to taste. Simmer on low for at least one hour, stirring occasionally to allow soup to thicken.

Servings: 10

Dick's Difficulty Gauge: Easy

Preparation Time:
Cooking Time: 1 hour and 20 minutes
Total Time: 1 hour and 20 minutes

Dicks Tips

If you don't feel like eating soup all week Dick, this one freezes well. Get yourself some of those single serving disposable plastic containers at the grocery store and freeze some bowls. When you get a hankering just thaw one out in the microwave.

COOKING WITH HOOCH

"I cook with wine, sometimes I even add it to the food."
~ W.C. Fields

Beer Me Cheddar Soup

This is a great soup with a little kick to serve on its own, or as an appetizer. Use your favorite beer Dick, but I would recommend sticking to the paler ales.

½ cup	Butter		½ tsp	White pepper
1 sm	Onion, grated		½ cup	All Purpose Flour
1	Garlic clove, minced		3 cups	Chicken broth
1 tsp	Worcestershire sauce		1¼ cups	Half and half cream
¾ tsp	Dry mustard		1 can	Beer
½ tsp	Cayenne pepper		4 cups	Sharp White Cheddar cheese, shredded
½ tsp	Salt		¼ cup	Parmesan cheese

Procedure

Using a large sauce pan (soup pot), melt butter on medium heat. Add onions and garlic and sauté for five minutes.

Next add Worcestershire, cayenne, mustard, salt and white pepper, cooking for an additional five minutes. Add the flour and stir constantly for one minute, until bubbling.

Gradually stir in the broth, cream and beer and cook until thickened, stirring constantly.

Add your cheeses and stir until melted. Reduce heat to low and simmer, stirring frequently until ready to serve. Try not to let the soup come to a full boil.

Servings: 8

Dick's Difficulty Gauge: Moderately difficult

Preparation Time:
Cooking Time: 30 minutes
Total Time: 30 minutes

Dicks Tips

When stirring in flour Dick, it tends to clump up. An easy trick to smooth things out is to use a wire whisk here instead of a spoon. Also, milk products will burn easily and stick to the bottom of the pan if the heat is too high and it sits too long. (And it's a nightmare to clean.) So have your final ingredients on hand, close to the stove so that you can stir the soup constantly.

Your mustard spice and will be in the spices section Dick. The Worcestershire and white pepper should already be in your cupboard since they're Dick Staples, but if not you'll find the Worcestershire in the condiments section by the sauces.

The Dick Factor: Fancy this up by serving with fresh parsley or some Dick's Croutons floating on the soup bowl.

Chili on a Bender

Okay Dick, this is a little more challenging...not hard, just time consuming but perfect for your Super Bowl Party. So grab yourself a couple of beers (one for you, one for the chili), put on some tunes and prepare to make a kick ass pot of chili.

3	cups	Six Month Mari-Me-Nara Sauce or alternate spaghetti sauce
1	can	Diced tomatoes - drained
1	can	Red Kidney Beans - rinsed and drained
1	can	Baked Brown Beans
1	can	Condensed Cream of Tomato soup
1	cup	Corn
¼	cup	Beef Bouillon concentrate (or five cubes)
¼	cup	Chili Pepper sauce
20	shakes	Frank's Red Hot sauce
10	shakes	Worcestershire sauce
10	shakes	Tabasco sauce
2	sqrs	Bakers Semi-sweet chocolate (trust me on this Dick)
2	tbsp	Butter
1	cup	Spanish Onion - chopped
1		Green pepper - chopped
1	cup	Mushrooms - chopped
4		Garlic cloves - crushed
1 ½	lbs	Lean ground beef
1	pkg	Chili Seasoning (Old El Paso is good)
1	can	Favorite Beer
½	lb	Bacon - chopped
		Salt and pepper to taste

Procedure

Combine sauce, tomatoes, beans, soup, corn, bouillon, chili pepper sauce, hot sauce, Worcestershire, Tabasco and chocolate in a large slow cooker turned to high. Cover and begin to warm.

Next melt the butter in a large frying pan on medium. Add onions, peppers, mushrooms and garlic then sauté for approximately ten minutes or until vegetables begin to soften.

Add ground beef and cook until browned.

Stir in chili seasoning and add your beer. Simmer on low for ten minutes and then transfer to the slow cooker, blending all ingredients.

Using the same pan, fry chopped bacon until golden, drain fat and transfer bacon to slow cooker.

Cook on high for at least four hours, then turn to low until ready to serve. Serve with garlic toast.

Servings: 10

Dick's Difficulty Gauge: Moderately difficult

Preparation Time: 1 hour
Cooking Time: 4 hours
Total Time: 5 hours

Dicks Tips

Make this in the morning Dick, as the longer it sits, the better it tastes. Also, you may want to freeze some left overs to use as The Dick Factor in Nascar Nachos.

Ciao Bella Steak

What could be more beautiful than a perfectly grilled steak with an exquisite portabella mushroom sauce? Here's hoping it's your dinner companion Dick.

4	Rib Eye Steaks	4	Garlic cloves, chopped or minced
1 tsp	Garlic powder		
	Montreal Steak Spice to taste	½ cup	Red or white wine
2 tbsp	Butter	2 cups	Portabella mushrooms, stem removed, washed and chopped (about 4 mushrooms)
2 tbsp	Olive oil		
2 med	Shallots, chopped		
		1 jar	Teriyaki sauce - ready to serve

Procedure

Sit your steaks out at room temperature for an hour or so Dick to get them ready for the barbecue. Season with garlic powder and Montreal Steak spice and set aside.

In a medium sized frying pan, melt butter and heat olive oil over medium heat.

Add the shallots and sauté for five minutes then add garlic and sauté for another minute.

Add the wine and mushrooms. Reducing heat slightly, boil softly for 7 - 10 minutes to reduce liquids.

Add the teriyaki sauce and heat through. Simmer on low until ready to serve, stirring occasionally.

Now grab yourself a drink and head for the barbecue with your steaks. Grill to your guests desires, then top with the portabella mushroom sauce and serve.

Servings: 4

Dick's Difficulty Gauge: Easy

Preparation Time: 10 minutes
Cooking Time: 30 minutes
Total Time: 40 minutes

Dicks Tips

To remove the stems from the portabella mushrooms gently wiggle the stem back and forth until you can gently remove it then toss it away. You don't need to remove the 'fins' - the black underbelly - but you can it if you'd like. Just shave them off with a spoon. Rinse and pat dry and they're ready to cook. For the teriyaki sauce, stay away from the 'marinades' and opt for the sauce or your mushroom sauce will be runny. Nobody likes runny sauce Dick.

Crabby Chicks

Oozing with creamy stuffed crab meat, this dish is sure to cheer up the grumpiest of diners. For a real tough case, just polish off the rest of the wine with dinner.

4	lg	Boneless, skinless chicken breasts
2	tbsp	Butter
2		Shallots, finely chopped
½	cup	Mushrooms, sliced
1½	tbsp	Flour
½	tsp	Dried thyme
½	cup	Chicken broth
¼	cup	Milk
¼	cup	Dry white wine
¼	cup	Swiss cheese, grated
½	cup	Imitation crab meat, chopped
¼	cup	Italian Style seasoned breadcrumbs
½	tsp	Dried dill

Procedure

Place chicken breasts in an empty clean grocery bag or large Ziploc bag and with a meat tenderizer pound to half their width. Set aside. Next, preheat oven to 325° F.

In a medium saucepan, melt butter over medium heat. Sauté shallots and mushrooms for ten minutes. Next stir in flour and thyme. Add chicken broth, milk, wine and cheese stirring constantly until mixture begins to boil and thickens. Remove from heat, cover and set aside.

Combine ¼ cup of the sauce with the crab meat, breadcrumbs and dill. Spoon equal parts of the crab mixture into the center of the chicken breasts. Roll chicken together and secure with a toothpick to keep rolled.

Spray a shallow baking dish with non-stick cooking spray, and arrange chicken, pouring remaining sauce over top. Bake uncovered for 45 minutes. Remove from oven and spoon warmed up sauce over top to serve.

Servings: 4

Dick's Difficulty Gauge: Moderately difficult

Oven Temperature: 325°F

Preparation Time: 45 minutes
Cooking Time: 45 minutes

Total Time: 1 hour and 30 minutes

Dicks Tips

You can find imitation crab meat at the seafood counter for pretty cheap Dick. Using the plastic bag to pound the chicken in will keep pieces of raw chicken from catapulting across the kitchen, and getting stuck in your meat tenderizer.

Fishing for Compliments

A very mild dish, bursting with flavor and sure to please. The presentation looks like you were hard at it in the kitchen, but preparation really is quite simple. Serve this with a side salad and some rice. Oh and Dick, don't forget the wine.

6 med	Tomatoes, chopped		1 tbsp	Herbs de Provence seasoning
1 med	Onion, chopped		1 tsp	Dried thyme
¼ cup	White wine		4 fillets	Tilapia
2 tbsp	Olive oil			Coarse Salt and Ground Black pepper

Procedure

Preheat oven to 375° F and lightly spray a 9" x 11" baking dish with cooking spray.

In the pan, mix tomatoes, onion, wine, olive oil and seasonings. Bake in the oven for 20 minutes.

Meanwhile in a large skillet, pan fry your Tilapia for about two minutes per side in a little bit of olive oil. Season with salt and pepper.

Carefully remove pan from the oven and space the fish fillets evenly in the pan. Spoon some of the tomato mixture on top. Place back in the oven and bake for an additional 20 minutes.

Servings: 4

Dick's Difficulty Gauge: Easy

Oven Temperature: 375°F

Preparation Time: 20 minutes
Cooking Time: 40 minutes
Total Time: 1 hour

Dicks Tips

You can substitute almost any white fish here Dick. Halibut and catfish are other options.

The Dick Factor: Instead of dried thyme, pick up some fresh thyme sprigs from the grocery store and use two of the sprigs for seasoning in the recipe. Use another four sprigs as garnish by placing one on top of each fish fillet just before serving. It's all about the presentation.

French Liqueur Chicken

Grand Marnier is a triple sec liqueur made in France with a fantastic orange flavor. Use it to cook with, then after dinner serve to guests in a warmed up brandy glass to really impress.

4		Boneless skinless chicken breasts	
3	tbsp	Flour	
1	tsp	White pepper	
1½	tsp	Paprika	
1	tsp	Garlic powder	
2	tbsp	Butter	
1	tbsp	Dijon mustard	
1	cup	Frozen orange juice concentrate	
¼	cup	Grand Marnier	
½	cup	Dry white wine	
2	tbsp	Flour	

Procedure

Preheat your oven to 350° F.

In a shallow pan, mix 2 tablespoons flour, pepper, paprika and garlic salt. Coat the chicken breasts with the flour mixture.

In a large skillet over medium heat, sauté the chicken breasts in 1 tablespoon of olive oil for about 2 minutes a side or until the outside is light brown.

Spray a medium sized baking pan or casserole dish with non-stick cooking spray and place the chicken breasts in it.

In a saucepan melt the butter then add the Dijon mustard, orange juice concentrate, Grand Marnier and white wine. Bring to a boil for 2-3 minutes.

Add 2 tablespoons flour and cook until mixture is slightly thickened and smooth. Whisk any lumps away.

Pour over chicken breasts, cover with a lid or tinfoil and bake for 40 minutes.

Servings: 4

Dick's Difficulty Gauge: Moderately difficult

Oven Temperature: 350°F

Preparation Time: 20 minutes
Cooking Time: 40 minutes

Total Time: 1 hour

Dicks Tips

A great side dish for this would be Rice Peel-Off Dick. Throw in a side salad, some wine, a little jazz music in the background and voila!

I'm a Catch Chicken Marsala

If you're still trying to convince her you're a keeper, one bite of this will close the deal. This dish is fan-friggin-tastic.

4-6		Boneless, skinless chicken breasts	2	tbsp	Olive oil
1	cup	Flour	1	lg	Spanish Onion - chopped
2	tsp	Garlic powder	5	cloves	Garlic, chopped or minced
1	tsp	Salt	1½	cups	Mushrooms, sliced
1	tsp	Black pepper	1	tbsp	Olive oil
2	tbsp	Butter	2	cups	Marsala wine

Procedure

Using a large Ziploc bag and your trusty meat tenderizer mallet, flatten the chicken breasts to about ¾ of their original size.

In a shallow dish, combine the flour, garlic, salt and pepper together. Coat each piece of chicken with the flour mixture then set aside.

In a large frying pan or better yet, a large electric skillet, melt butter and olive oil together on medium-high heat. Add the shallots and sauté for five minutes.

Next add your garlic and mushrooms, continuing to cook until mushrooms start to soften.

Remove the onion and mushroom mixture and temporarily place in a separate dish, covering to keep warm.

In the same pan, add another tablespoon of olive oil and heat on medium-high. Add the chicken breasts and cook for about three minutes per side, just lightly browning the coating.

Now return the mushroom mixture back to the pan, and add the Marsala Wine. The wine should come up to the tops of the chicken but not cover them completely.

Bring the Marsala Wine to a boil then reduce heat and simmer on medium-low to allow the Marsala to thicken. Depending on how much wine you need, this should take about 20 minutes Dick.

Remove the chicken from the pan and serve with additional mushroom sauce poured on top.

Servings: 4

Yield: 4 - 6 Chicken Breasts

Dick's Difficulty Gauge: Moderately difficult

Dicks Tips

You will have to head for the liquor store and likely ask the staff to point you in the direction of the Marsala wine Dick. This will be the only time I tell you to choose the sweet variety over the dry. The sweet Marsala wine is what really makes this dish, but of course it's all about personal preference

Carb-a-Palooza Potato Casserole is good side for this dish along with a simple veggie like green beans.

Marg Or Rita Chicken

Can't seem to make up your mind Dick? Throw together this chicken dish, marinated in tequila and have them both over. To the victor go the spoils!

4	Boneless, skinless chicken breasts	2 tbsp	Grand Marnier
½ cup	Lime juice, freshly squeezed	1 tbsp	Liquid honey
½ cup	Golden tequila	2	Garlic cloves, minced
¼ cup	Olive oil		Salt and pepper to taste

Procedure

Preheat your oven to 425° F.

In an extra-large Ziploc bag or glass bowl, combine all liquid ingredients.

With your meat tenderizer, lightly pound the chicken. Add to the mixture, cover and marinade over night, or for at least 3 hours.

Transfer marinade to a small sauce pan to use later.

Wrap each of your chicken breasts in aluminum foil and place on a cookie sheet and bake for 25 minutes.

Remove from oven and allow to sit for an additional 10 minutes.

Meanwhile, over medium high heat, bring your marinade to a boil. Unwrap chicken then drizzle a small amount of marinade over top and serve.

Servings: 4

Dick's Difficulty Gauge: Easy

Oven Temperature: 425°F

Preparation Time: 3 hours
Cooking Time: 30 minutes
Total Time: 3 hours and 30 minutes

Dicks Tips

Tenderizing the chicken slightly will produce super tender, moist meat and it's a manly Dick tool that lets you whack something while cooking. Just don't pulverize it

Dick…a few good whacks per side ought to do it. To keep the mess down, place the chicken into a plastic grocery bag and then pound. As for the Grand Marnier, this orange flavored liqueur is great to keep on hand for after dinner drinks and recipes.

Mojo-Mojito Shrimp

Harness your inner Mojo with this perfect summer recipe and strut your stuff. You got this Dick.

15	Fresh mint leaves	1 tsp	Sea salt
½	cup Rum	4 lbs	Shrimp - extra-large or jumbo size, raw, shells removed
¼	cup Lime juice		
2	tbsp Sugar	1 can	Pineapple chunks (or fresh pineapple if its available)

Procedure

Coarsely chop your mint leaves and place in a large glass bowl. Take a spoon and crush some of the leaves to release the juices.

Add rum, lime juice, sugar and salt. Stir thoroughly to ensure the salt dissolves.

Add the shrimp, toss to coat and let sit in the marinade for no longer than 20 minutes.

Remove shrimp and reserve the marinade for basting.

Thread the shrimp onto your skewers with a large pineapple chunk between each one.

Heat the barbecue up to medium-high heat. Grill the skewers directly on the grill, basting with the reserved marinade and turning occasionally until pink in colour and no longer opaque. This should take between 5 and 10 minutes depending on the size of your shrimp.

Remove from heat, drizzle a little more marinade on them and serve immediately.

Servings: 4

Dick's Difficulty Gauge: Easy

Preparation Time: 30 minutes
Cooking Time: 7 minutes
Total Time: 37 minutes

Dicks Tips

As with all seafood and fish, fresh ingredients are a must here Dick. Gently peel the shells off and rinse shrimp thoroughly with cold water before marinating. Make sure you grab yourself some decent sized shrimp as there is no room for the little guys in this recipe.

Rice Peel Off will go well with this meal.

On Tap Guinness Stew

No beer was harmed in the making of this recipe. Guinness not only adds a distinct flavor but it helps tenderize the beef as well.

3 tbsp	Olive oil		2 tsp	Herbs de Provence seasoning
2 tbsp	Butter		3 tsp	Flour
2 lbs	Stewing beef cut into bite sized cubes, about 2 inches		¾ cup	Beef broth or stock
			½ cup	Guinness Stout
1 lg	Spanish onion, chopped into bite sized pieces		½ lb	Carrots, chopped
				Coarse salt and ground pepper to taste
3	Garlic cloves, chopped			
2 tbsp	Tomato paste			
1 tbsp	Water			

Procedure

Preheat oven to 300° F.

In a large oven proof pot (Dutch oven), heat oil and butter on medium high heat. Add beef and brown on all sides. Add the onions and garlic, then sauté for approximately five minutes.

Reduce heat to medium. Mix the tomato paste with the water to dilute and add to the pot along with the Herbs de Provence and flour, blending well.

Reduce heat to medium-low and add the beef stock and Guinness, cooking for about 15 minutes or until mixture slightly thickens.

Add the remaining ingredients, cover and bake in the oven at 300° for two hours.

Servings: 6

Dick's Difficulty Gauge: Moderately difficult

Oven Temperature: 300°F

Preparation Time: 30 minutes
Cooking Time: 2 hours
Total Time:

Dicks Tips

As with all beef I recommend you warm your cubes up to room temperature Dick to promote tenderness. Leave on the counter for a good hour before throwing them in the pot.

Whip up some Wine & Cheese Biscuits to serve with this stew.

Seducer Sambuca Shrimp and Scallops

Okay Dick, time for the big leagues. This one you actually get to set on fire...really. Don't be scared off, just follow the instructions carefully and you'll look like a pro in the kitchen!

2 tbsp	Butter, melted		½ lb	Fresh scallops
½ cup	Half and half cream		¼ cup	Shallots, finely chopped
2	Garlic cloves, minced		½ lb	Large cooked shrimp
8 cups	Cooked linguine		2oz	Sambuca liqueur
2 tbsp	Butter			Salt and pepper to taste

Procedure

In a container mix melted butter, cream and garlic together. Refrigerate for an hour or more to allow the garlic to flavor the cream.

Cook linguine according to package directions, then drain, cover and set aside to keep warm.

In a large skillet, melt additional butter over medium heat. Add shallots and scallops then sauté for five minutes. Next add shrimp and sauté for an additional five minutes.

Now for the fun part. Turn the heat up to medium high for one minute. Now using a shot glass (not the bottle Dick) add your Sambuca to the pan and shake the pan to coat shrimp and scallops. Using a barbecue lighter, ignite the Sambuca near the outside edge of the pan. (Think Flaming Sambuca shots.) Once food ignites, allow Sambuca to burn off. Be careful for the love of God and don't set the kitchen on fire.

Reduce heat to medium low, and add cream mixture. Stir constantly, simmering for five minutes until sauce thickens. Season with salt and pepper to suit taste.

Rinse and strain pasta with hot water to reheat noodles, then arrange on your plates. Pour the cream mixture from the skillet over noodles and serve immediately.

Servings: 6

Dick's Difficulty Gauge: Moderately difficult

Preparation Time: 20 minutes
Cooking Time: 45 minutes
Inactive Time: 1 hour
Total Time: 2 hours and 5 minutes

Dicks Tips

To cook up the right amount of pasta, try to measure about 3/4 of an inch dry per person. So for four people Dick, you're looking at a 3 inch bundle of linguine.

As for flambéing Dick, please be careful. Don't stand over the pan when you ignite, and don't pour directly from the bottle. Also, if you're using a gas stove, remove pan from heat prior to setting your Sambuca ablaze. We don't want to burn the place down.

The Dick Factor: For presentation Dick, get yourself some fresh parsley or rosemary to garnish the tops of the plates. Accompany with some Dicks Garlic Bread.

Slow Cooker Beef au Beer Sandwiches

You don't need a fancy roast here Dick as the slow cooker (crock-pot) will make tender almost any cut of beef. This will serve a lot of people and would be a good choice for a house-full of buddies over for poker or the game. Or just because they found out you're cooking tonight.

- 4 lbs Sirloin roast
- 1 pkg Lipton's Onion Roasted Garlic soup mix
- 1 can Beer
- 2 tbsp Butter
- 2 large Spanish onions, sliced
- 2 cups Sliced mushrooms
- Fresh Kaiser buns
- Swiss and marble cheese slices

Procedure

Place the roast into a crock-pot and sprinkle the soup mix over top. Pour beer over roast, cover and cook on low for seven hours, or until roast easily falls apart. Baste occasionally with the juices.

Just before serving, melt butter over medium heat in a large sauce pan, and add onions. Cook for about ten minutes. Add mushrooms and cook for an additional ten minutes, or until soft.

Cut or pull the meat apart to use for sandwiches. Stack the Kaisers with meat, onions and mushrooms, and cheese of choice.

Using small bowls, ladle some of the drippings (au jus) into single serving bowls and serve as a dip for the sandwiches.

Servings: 10

Dick's Difficulty Gauge: Easy

Preparation Time: 25 minutes
Cooking Time: 5 hours
Total Time: 5 hours

Dicks Tips

Serve with a side of Wicked Wedges for a complete meal. Be sure to save any leftover meat and au jus as this reheats quite easily.

That's the Spirit Pork Tenderloin

Bourbon whiskey is a barrel-aged distilled spirit made from corn Dick, but sadly doesn't count toward your daily dose of vegetables. The use of both bourbon and red wine in this recipe will certainly give you a new appreciation for that fine Kentucky spirit.

2 tbsp	Butter	1½ cups	Beef broth or stock
1 tbsp	Olive oil	¼ cup	Bourbon
2 med	Shallots, finely chopped	½ cup	Half and half cream
4 cloves	Garlic, chopped	1 tbsp	Butter
2 cups	Cremini Mushrooms, sliced	1 lb	Pork tenderloin - seasoned all over with garlic powder and black pepper
1 cup	Red wine		
2 tsp	Herbes de Provence seasoning		

Procedure

In a large skillet on medium heat sauté shallots, garlic, and mushrooms in the butter and olive oil for about 10 minutes, browning just slightly.

Add the wine and Herbes de Provence seasoning and increase the heat to high. Softly boil on medium low for five minutes to reduce the wine.

Next throw in the chicken broth and bourbon, continuing to softly boil for another 10 minutes.

Finally add the cream and simmer 5 - 10 minutes or until the sauce thickens. Simmer on low to keep warm stirring occasionally.

In another large frying pan, add the butter and heat over medium-high. Take the tenderloin and brown all over - about 1 -2 minutes per side.

Remove the pork from the pan and after cooling for a few minutes slice the tenderloin into medallions - about 1½" thick.

Return the medallions to the pan and cook over medium heat for 3 - 4 minutes per side.

Arrange medallions on your plates and pour a generous portion of the sauce over top.

Servings: 4

Dick's Difficulty Gauge: Moderately difficult

Preparation Time: 10 minutes
Cooking Time: 50 minutes
Total Time: 1 hour

Dicks Tips

You'll find the fresh cremini mushrooms with the rest of their peeps in the mushroom section Dick. You can also substitute regular or button mushrooms if need be.

Thighs of Rum & Coconut

Not sure if you're ready to spend a week on an island? Serve up some coconut chicken along with enough rum to make you both think you're already there.

4½ lbs Chicken thighs, skins removed (about 12 pieces)	¼ cup Lime juice, freshly squeezed if you can swing it
½ cup Coconut rum	¼ cup Honey
¼ cup Soy sauce	2 cups Sweetened shredded coconut

Procedure

If you didn't buy the skinless thighs at the grocery store Dick, remove the skins and discard. Take a fork and pierce the chicken thighs with a few pokes each to allow for better absorption of the marinade.

In a large glass bowl or extra-large zip-lock bag, combine the rum, soy, lime juice and honey making sure the ingredients are well blended.

Place the chicken in the marinade and soak in the refrigerator for 1 - 3 hours.

Preheat oven to 375° F.

Remove chicken and place the marinade in a small sauce pot.

Place the coconut flakes in a shallow dish and coat each piece of chicken thoroughly with the coconut.

Arrange chicken on a cookie sheet that you've liberally sprayed with non-stick cooking spray and bake for 45 minutes.

About 20 minutes before the chicken is done, heat up your reserved marinade on medium high and boil gently for 10 minutes, reducing to a simmer to keep warm.

Remove the chicken from the oven and lightly drizzle the chicken with the cooked marinade.

Servings: 4
Yield: 12 pieces

Dick's Difficulty Gauge: Easy

Oven Temperature: 375°F

Dicks Tips

You can always grill these on the barbecue instead Dick and they will taste just as great. Just be careful not to handle the thighs too much - you're coconut will take a beating.

Jacked Meat

This is about as easy as it gets Dick. Three ingredients and some meat...done.

½ cup	Jack Daniel's Whiskey	½ cup	Sugar
½ cup	Soy Sauce	4 pcs	Chicken breasts...or steak...or pork...whatever Dick.

Procedure

Dump all three ingredients for sauce into a large Ziploc bag.

Place your choice of meat (chicken, pork, beef or salmon) into the Ziploc bag with marinade and refrigerate for at least one hour.

Cook meat as desired, although this is a great marinade for the barbecue. Serve with your favorite sides.

Servings: 4

Dick's Difficulty Gauge: Very easy

Preparation Time: 5 minutes
Cooking Time: 20 minutes
Inactive Time: 1 hour
Total Time: 1 hour and 25 minutes

Dicks Tips

If you choose steaks for this recipe, allow them to warm to room temperature either during or after marinating before you cook them. This will really increase tenderness.

BACK OF THE LINE BOYS…SHE'S ALL MINE

"Cooking is like love:
It should be entered into with abandon or not at all."
~ Harriet van Horne

Big Balls Spaghetti

You gotta have balls to admit when you're wrong Dick, but sometimes it's worth it. Here's a recipe for some home-made meatballs that you can whip-up and then add to the Six Month Mari-Me-Nara Sauce for some man-sized spaghetti.

¼ cup	Chopped cooking onions		1 tbsp	Herbes de Provence
1 tbsp	Butter		½ cup	Grated parmesan cheese
2 lbs	Lean ground beef		1 tsp	Garlic powder
2	Eggs, beaten		1 tsp	Salt
¾ cup	Seasoned Italian breadcrumbs		1 tsp	Pepper

Procedure

Preheat oven to 325° F.

In a small frying pan on medium heat, sauté the chopped onions in the butter for about ten minutes, or until soft.

In a large bowl mix together all ingredients, including cooked onions and work the mixture through with your hands until well blended.

Roll meat mixture into large, good sized meatballs, about 3 inches in diameter. You should have about 18 meatballs or so. Place on a broiler pan (which helps catch dripping's) and bake for 40 minutes.

Once cooked, simmer the meatballs in a pot of Six Month Marinara Sauce for about an hour. Serve over your favorite spaghetti.

Servings: 8
Yield: 18 Meatballs

Dick's Difficulty Gauge: Easy

Oven Temperature: 325°F

Preparation Time: 30 minutes
Cooking Time: 40 minutes
Total Time: 1 hour and 10 minutes

Dicks Tips

If you don't have a broiler pan Dick, or you want to display some REALLY big balls, you can use a muffin tin instead. As for the pasta, the effect here is really pulled off with a big plate of good old fashioned spaghetti. Serve with Dicks Bread n' Butter and some wine, and hopefully you'll be out of the dog house before desert.

Bombshell Burrito's

While this isn't your classic burrito recipe Dick, it's pretty damn good.

2 lbs	Lean ground beef	1 pkg	Large (10-inch) flour tortilla shells (about 10 shells)
1 cup	Water	1 large	Tomato, chopped
2 pkg's	Burrito Seasoning Mix	1 bunch	Green onions, chopped
½ cup	Salsa		
1 pkg	Cream cheese - room temperature		
2 cups	Mexican blend or Jalapeño Monterey Jack cheese - divided in half		

Procedure

In a large skillet brown the lean ground beef over medium heat until no longer pink. Drain off the fat and return to the stove.

Add the water and Burrito Seasoning mix to the ground beef, and stir until well blended.

Next throw in the salsa and cook over medium heat until most of the moisture in the meat mixture is cooked off, about 10 minutes.

Next pull the cream cheese apart into smaller sections and add to the pan, followed by one cup of the shredded cheese. Reduce heat to medium-low and simmer for 20 minutes, stirring regularly to melt and combine all the cheese.

Once your mixture has reached a thick porridge like consistency, remove from heat and allow to cool for 15 minutes.

Preheat oven to 350° F.

Spray a 13" x 9" baking pan with cooking spray.

Taking your soft tortilla shells, carefully spoon a couple of scoops of the meat mixture into the center of the shell. Wrap it up and place in the baking sheet. Repeat until all of your shells are full.

Take any remaining meat sauce and pour over the arranged burritos.

Sprinkle the remaining cup of shredded cheese on top, followed by the chopped tomato and green onion.

Place baking pan into the center of the oven and bake uncovered for 30 minutes,

Remove from oven, allow to sit for 5 minutes and serve. This will be hot Dick so careful.

Servings: 5
Yield: 10 Burrito's

Dick's Difficulty Gauge: Moderately difficult

Oven Temperature: 350°F

Preparation Time: 1 hour
Cooking Time: 30 minutes
Total Time: 1 hour and 30 minutes

Dicks Tips

Make sure to have some sour cream and salsa to serve on the side with these Dick. Sticking to lean ground beef and whole wheat tortilla shells makes this a wee bit better for you and won't compromise on taste. That being said, no-one eats burritos for the health of it.

You can also substitute regular shredded marble cheese in the recipe if you like it on the milder side. Whatever floats your boat Dick.

Crazy Chick Salad

Chicks love their salads Dick so you may as well make one you'll both enjoy. This one's loaded with protein and veggies, still lets you work the barbecue and will work just fine as a standalone meal.

2	boneless skinless chicken breasts	½	Cucumber, sliced
1	Oktoberfest sausage	1 lg	Tomato, chopped
1 tsp	Garlic Powder	½ med	Red onion, thinly sliced
1 tsp	Cajun seasoning	½ cup	Shredded cheddar cheese, old
4 cups	Romaine lettuce, washed, dried and cut into bite sized pieces		

Procedure

Spark up the barbee Dick - medium heat oughta do it.

Season your chicken breasts with some garlic powder and Cajun seasoning. Place the chicken and the Oktoberfest sausage on the barbecue and cook until done, turning occasionally - about 15 minutes.

Wash and dry your romaine lettuce. (This would be a good time to try out that salad spinner I suggested you buy for Dick's Tool Box.)

Combine romaine, cucumber, tomato and onion to make yourself an old school chef salad. Spread out on two plates.

Top each of the salads with half of the shredded old cheddar.

Slice the chicken and the sausage and spread evenly (or not) on top of the salad and cheese.

That's it Dick. You're done. Serve supersized with your dressing of choice and you've got yourself a man-salad.

Servings: 2

Dick's Difficulty Gauge: Easy

Preparation Time: 15 minutes
Cooking Time: 15 minutes
Total Time: 30 minutes

Dicks Tips

You can substitute any meat here pal. Grilled steak, ham, salmon - you name it. You can even get a little crazy with the cheese. Just make sure you have fresh ingredients and big plates.

Cooking for one? Just halve the recipe Dick.

Crème de la Femmes Salmon

If she is in fact the crème-de-la-crème, then serve her this dish to show her you know how good you've got it. You go Dick.

1	lb	Salmon fillet, or enough for two people	½ cup	Light cream
1	tbsp	Olive oil	¼ cup	Capers drained
1	tbsp	Butter	2 tbsp	Basil Pesto
3	lg	Shallots, peeled and chopped fine	1 tbsp	Lemon juice
2		Garlic cloves, minced		Ground pepper and salt to taste
¾	cup	Dry white wine		

Procedure

Rinse salmon with cold water then cut in half.

In a large fry pan, melt butter over medium-high heat. Add salmon pieces and sear for about 3 to 4 minutes a side depending on how well you like your salmon cooked. Remove from pan to another dish and cover with aluminum foil to keep warm.

Using the same pan, add shallots and garlic and sauté for 5 minutes. Stir frequently.

Next, add the remaining ingredients to the pan, stirring constantly over medium heat until mixture thickens and reduces. This should take about 15-20 minutes.

Place salmon on a plate, and pour sauce over each fillet.

Servings: 2

Dick's Difficulty Gauge: Easy

Preparation Time: 10 minutes
Cooking Time: 30 minutes
Total Time: 40 minutes

Dicks Tips

When picking out your salmon, stick with fresh fillets from the fish counter. Avoid the salmon steaks, as they often have bones which are not cool for a romantic dinner. The Dick Factor: Garnish salmon with a sprig of parsley for a nice presentation. Serve with a rice dish and salad for a wonderful setting.

Flex Your Mussels

Show her what you've got Dick. Even if you're not a world class body builder, you can flex your stuff in the kitchen.

2½ lbs	Fresh mussels		3 cloves	Garlic, minced
¼ cup	Coarse Salt		2 med	Tomatoes, chopped
¼ cup	Flour		1 tsp	Oregano
2 tbsp	Olive oil			Coarse salt and ground black pepper to taste
2 tbsp	Butter			
3 tbsp	Onion, minced		½ cup	Dry white wine
			1	Baguette

Procedure

Wash and rinse mussels in cold water. Using a small knife, remove beards. (Not your beard Dick, and hopefully not hers. See directions below.)

Soak mussels for about 30 minutes in cold water containing coarse salt and flour.

In a medium sized sauce pan add olive oil and melt butter over medium heat. Sauté onions for ten minutes or until soft. Next add garlic and sauté for one more minute.

Add tomato, oregano, salt and pepper and cook for fifteen minutes until tomato begins to soften.

Add wine and bring to a boil over medium low heat. Add drained and rinsed mussels then cover and steam for six to eight minutes, stirring occasionally until mussels open.

Discard any mussels that don't open. Serve the rest in bowls with some of the broth drizzled over. Serve with a freshly sliced baguette.

Servings: 4

Dick's Difficulty Gauge: Moderately difficult

Preparation Time: 30 minutes
Cooking Time: 35 minutes
Total Time: 1 hour and 5 minutes

Dicks Tips

Check out your mussels before soaking them Dick. They should be closed tight - discard any that are already cracked open. Soaking the mussels in salt and flour will remove any leftover sand from the mussels.

You may see what looks like brown stringy seaweed hanging out of some of the shells. This is what we refer to as the beard. Nobody likes hair in their food, so simply grab the mussel, pinch the beard tightly with your fingers and tug on it until it comes out. Clean shaven mussels Dick - that's our goal.

Fromage et Deux Jumbo Shells

Nothing says true love like a nice set of stuffed shells.

25		Jumbo Pasta Shells	
2	tbsp	Butter	
1	med	Spanish onion, finely chopped	
3		Garlic cloves, minced	
1	lb	Ground turkey	
2	cups	Light ricotta cheese (fromage et une)	
1½	cups	Mozzarella cheese, shredded (fromage et deux)	
1	pkg	Frozen chopped spinach, thawed and squeezed dry (300 g)	
1	tsp	Herbes de Provence spice	
		Salt and pepper to taste	
4	cups	Six Month Mari-Me-Nara Sauce or other spaghetti sauce	

Procedure

Cook pasta shells according to package directions. Rinse, strain and set aside.

Preheat oven to 350° F.

In a large frying pan over medium heat, melt butter and sauté onions for 5 minutes. Add garlic and sauté for an additional minute.

Next throw in the ground turkey and fry for about 10 minutes, or until meat is no longer pink and the water in the pan has evaporated. Be sure to break up ground meat as you fry to keep it loose.

Remove from heat and stir in ricotta, half of mozzarella, spinach and spices being sure to combine well. Allow to cool slightly before handling.

Spray a 13" x 9" baking pan with cooking spray and spread 2 cups of the pasta sauce onto the bottom of a large baking dish.

Scoop about 2 tablespoons of meat mixture into shells and arrange stuffed shells over bottom layer of sauce. Pour the remaining sauce over pasta shells, then top with remaining mozzarella cheese.

Bake uncovered for 30 minutes. Remove from oven and allow to sit for 5 minutes before serving.

Servings: 6

Yield: 25 Stuffed Shells

Dick's Difficulty Gauge: Moderately difficult

Preparation Time: 50 minutes
Cooking Time: 30 minutes
Total Time: 1 hour and 20 minutes

Dicks Tips

You'll probably find about 40 shells in a box Dick. You may want to cook them all, as some are sure to tear. If you've got extra shells and meat mixture left, stuff 'em and freeze 'em for later. Alternatively, throw leftover meat mixture in the fridge and use it for an omelet stuffing in the morning!

You can use regular or lean ground beef instead of the turkey as well, although the turkey is a healthier choice. If you do substitute, be sure to drain off any excess fat.

Fuhgeddaboudit Prime Rib

Nothing is better than a perfectly cooked Prime Rib. Well...almost nothing. Anyway, this recipe is your ace up your sleeve, involves very little skill and quite frankly, impossible to screw up if you follow these simple directions.

6-9	lb	Prime Rib roast	1	tbsp	Garlic powder (not salt Dick, powder)
2	cups	Water			
1	cup	Red wine	1	tbsp	Fine black pepper
1	pkg	Lipton Onion Roasted Garlic Soup Mix	5-6	sprigs	Rosemary
			2	cups	Beef broth or stock
2	tbsp	Olive oil			

Procedure

- The first step here is a must Dick. Take your Prime Rib out of the fridge and warm it up to room temperature for at least 3 hours. You don't want a cold roast going into that oven. Kapeesh?
- Okay, when you're ready to start remove the middle rack from the oven, and preheat to 500° F.
- You will need your roasting pan and drip rack for this. Mix the water, red wine and soup mix in the bottom of the roasting pan and once combined put the drip pan in. Don't try to do this without the drip pan Dick. It won't be pretty.
- Rub the entire roast with olive oil.
- Mix the garlic powder and pepper together and rub into the roast, covering all of the meat.
- Place the roast bone side down into the pan, on the drip rack. Arrange the rosemary along the top of the roast and place a leave-in digital meat thermometer into the center of the roast.
- Once your oven has reached 500° F place the roast in the oven and cook for 20 minutes. Use a timer for this Dick as you don't want to go over 20 minutes.
- When you've hit 20 minutes, turn the oven down to 200° F and just walk away Dick. Don't go opening the door or messing with anything. Just fuhgeddaboudit.
- Leave your roast to slowly cook for the rest of the day, about 6 hours.

Turn the oven back up to 350° about twenty minutes before you remove the roast, to bring the internal temperature up. Keep an eye on the thermometer reading and remove the roast 5 degrees sooner than your desired doneness level. (See Dick's Doneness Chart for meat temperatures.)

Remove the roast and wrap in tinfoil. Leave it sit on the counter for 20 - 30 minutes. Don't rush this step either Dick as you want the juices to redistribute evenly.

For the au jus put the pan on the stove top and bring the dripping's to a boil adding the beef broth. Reduce heat and simmer to keep warm.

All you have left to do is carve that baby up, drizzle with some au jus and serve. Nicely done Dick.

Servings: 8
Yield: Makes 6 - 8 servings.

Dick's Difficulty Gauge: Easy

Oven Temperature: 200°F

Preparation Time: 15 minutes
Cooking Time: 6 hours
Inactive Time: 30 minutes
Total Time: 6 hours and 45 minutes

Dicks Tips

Serve this with some Bare Naked Garlic Mashed Potatoes and Asparadick & Hollandaise for a truly fine dining experience in your own kitchen.

Dick Factor: A nice bottle of Cabernet Sauvignon would go well with this meal Dick and shoot for a classy table setting.

Hide the Salami Baked Chicken

Time for a little game of Hide the Salami? This recipe can put anyone in the mood.

4	Boneless skinless chicken breasts	8 slices	Salami, 2" in diameter, thinly sliced
½ pkg	Cream cheese, room temperature (4 ounces)		Coarse ground pepper
		2 tbsp	olive oil
10 med	Olives, Manzanilla stuffed with pimento, chopped		Cooking spray
1 tsp	Garlic powder		

Procedure

Preheat oven to 375° F.

In a small bowl, mix together cream cheese, olives and garlic powder.

With a sharp knife, slice a pocket into the side of the chicken breasts, going as deep as possible without cutting through all the way. Picture an envelope Dick, open only on the one side.

Lay two pieces of the salami inside of the chicken, overlapping slightly and lying flat for now.

With a small spoon, stuff approximately one tablespoon of the cream cheese mixture into the back of the chicken breast (bottom of the envelope) but on top of the salami. Then carefully fold the section of salami that's sticking out of the chicken into the chicken breast, over top of the cream cheese mixture. It should seal the cream cheese mixture in between the chicken breast and salami.

Sprinkle the chicken breasts with coarse black pepper to taste. (Skip the salt here Dick as the salami and olives are salty enough).

In a large skillet type frying pan, heat up the olive oil on medium high heat. Place the chicken breasts in, pepper side down, and brown for about three minutes. Sprinkle pepper on the unseasoned side, and then flip over and brown for another three minutes.

Spray a large baking dish with cooking spray and then transfer the chicken to this pan. Bake at 375° F for 25 minutes.

Remove from oven and let cool for ten minutes before serving.

Servings: 4

Dick's Difficulty Gauge: Moderately difficult

Oven Temperature: 375°F

Preparation Time: 30 minutes
Cooking Time: 25 minutes
Total Time: 1 hour and 35 minutes

Dicks Tips

Don't let this recipe scare you off because it really is as easy as following each step. Once you stuff your first breast you'll be good to go. Try to find a milder tasting salami if you can. Just ask at the deli counter for some help. As for the chicken itself, serve this with something mild tasting such as rice or potatoes.

Honey I'm Home Pork Chops

You catch more flies with honey than vinegar Dick. What the hell does that mean anyway? While you're likely not interested in catching flies, you are interested in catching praise for your culinary skills. This is so easy yet so good and versatile for grill or oven.

¼ cup	Lemon juice (freshly squeezed if you have it on hand)	3		Garlic cloves, minced
¼ cup	Honey	2 tbsp	Ginger, minced
3	Green onions, chopped	2 tbsp	Olive oil
3 tbsp	Soya Sauce - Low Sodium	6		pork chops, about an inch thick

Procedure

Combine all ingredients except the pork chops in a shallow dish, or better yet a sealable Ziploc bag. Stir/shake to combine.

Add the pork chops to the Ziploc bag and marinate in the refrigerator for 1 to 2 hours, or overnight.

Remove the pork chops and reserve some of the marinade. Grill the pork chops on the barbecue over medium-high heat for about 15 minutes, turning once, basting occasionally with the reserved marinade.

Remove from heat and serve.

Servings: 4
Yield: 4 - 6 Pork Chops

Dick's Difficulty Gauge: Very easy

Preparation Time: 10 minutes
Cooking Time: 15 minutes
Inactive Time: 1 hour
Total Time: 1 hour and 25 minutes

Dicks Tips

If you prefer Dick, you can always throw these in the oven. Spray a baking sheet with non-stick cooking spray and bake at 375° F for 30 - 40 minutes depending on the thickness of your chops.

If you want a cheat factor - grab a jar of honey garlic cooking sauce and add ginger and onion. Though I can assure you it won't be as good.

Dick Factor: Want to look really cool? Slice a couple of peaches in half and grill alongside on the barbecue to serve with the pork chops, and top with a sprig of rosemary. Ohhh ya.

Man Up Sausage Manicotti

There comes a point in every Dick's life where he's just gotta man up. Do it with grace and manicotti Dick.

12		Manicotti shells	¼	cup	Parmesan cheese
4		Italian sausage, casings removed and chopped	2	cups	Ricotta cheese
			1		Egg beaten
2	sm	Shallots, finely chopped	3	cups	Six Month Mari-Me-Nara Sauce or alternate spaghetti sauce
½	cup	Dry white wine			
1	tbsp	Herbs de Provence seasoning	1	cup	Mozzarella cheese shredded
1	pkg	Frozen chopped spinach, thawed and squeezed dry			

Procedure

In a large pot, bring water to a boil and cook manicotti shells according to package directions, or until just softened. Rinse with cool water and set aside.

Preheat oven to 350° F.

In a large frying pan, cook sausage and shallots over medium heat, breaking up sausage into a crumbly mixture as you go until lightly browned.

Once browned, add white wine and Herbs de Provence, then cook until wine is reduced - approximately five minutes. Remove from heat and let stand.

In a separate mixing bowl, combine spinach, parmesan, ricotta and egg. Mix thoroughly.

Now add your sausage Dick. Mix it again until all ingredients are thoroughly combined.

Find yourself a 13" x 9" baking dish and spray that bad boy with some cooking spray. Spread one cup of spaghetti sauce onto the bottom of the pan.

Now you need to fill the shells Dick. Using your hands or a small spoon, gently stuff the sausage mixture into the cooled manicotti shells until just full. Place each stuffed shell in the baking dish.

Spread the remaining two cups of spaghetti sauce over the manicotti shells, then cover with some tin foil.

Bake at 350° F for 40 minutes, then remove and discard foil. Sprinkle shredded mozzarella cheese onto manicotti then return to oven for another 15 minutes or until cheese is melted and bubbly.

Remove from oven and let sit five to ten minutes before serving.

Servings: 6

Dick's Difficulty Gauge: Moderately difficult

Oven Temperature: 350°F

Preparation Time: 45 minutes
Cooking Time: 1 hour
Total Time: 1 hour and 45 minutes

Dicks Tips

Good quality cheese will ensure you pull this off flawlessly Dick. For a twist, substitute hot Italian sausage for the regular stuff and sprinkle with shredded smoked Gouda cheese instead of regular mozzarella.

Mari-Me-Nara Spaghetti with Meatballs and Sausage

You'll find the Six Month Mari-Me-Nara Sauce recipe in Dicks Staples. While any meat will do, this is especially great when you add some meatballs and sausage to the mix. Serve up with Dicks Caesar Salad, Garlic Bread and wine - and the only thing you'll be missing is a good episode of the Soprano's.

8 cups	Six Month Mari-Me-Nara Sauce	1 tbsp	Olive oil
2 cups	Pre-cooked Frozen Meatballs	1 box	Rotini Pasta - or any pasta you choose Dick.
4	Oktoberfest Sausage, chopped		

Procedure

In a large pot, heat up approximately 8 cups of Six Month Mari-Me-Nara Sauce on medium heat, turning down to a simmer once it starts to bubble.

Meanwhile, thaw out approximately a half package of frozen meatballs in the microwave for about five minutes. On this note, grab some balls worth serving Dick - the meatier the better.

Take your Oktoberfest Sausage, thaw and slice into medallions.

Add the meatballs and sausage to your sauce and continue to simmer for at least another 45 minutes.

In a separate pot, bring 8 cups of water to a boil, adding a tbsp of olive oil to the water. Boil your pasta to your desired 'doneness' ensuring not to overcook. Drain then rinse with hot water.

Spoon your sauce over your favourite pasta.

Servings: 8
Yield: Approximately 10 Cups

Dick's Difficulty Gauge: Easy

Preparation Time: 15 minutes
Cooking Time:
Total Time: 1 hour

Dicks Tips

What the hell is pesto and where do you find it? It's a paste like sauce normally made from fresh basil, garlic, olive oil, and parmesan cheese. It can be found at the grocery store where spaghetti sauces are located. Look near the top shelf Dick, as the jars are generally small. It's also a Dick Staple so be sure to keep it on hand. This sauce is a sure fire hit Dick and can be used as a base sauce for most any pasta dish, or on the side as a dip with some fresh garlic bread.

Nice Rack...of Lamb

Still in search of the perfect rack Dick? Look no further, the journey ends here.

½ cup	Italian seasoned bread crumbs	1 rack	Lamb - 7 to 8 bones (allow to sit at room temperature for an hour before cooking Dick)
2 tbsp	Garlic, chopped or minced		
½ tsp	Black pepper		
4 tbsp	Olive oil	2 tbsp	Dijon mustard
1 med	Shallot, chopped		

Procedure

Okay Dick here we go. Move your oven rack to the center of the oven and preheat to 450° F.

Grab a large bowl and combine the Italian bread crumbs, garlic, pepper and 2 tablespoons of olive oil.

Next, in a large oven proof skillet heat up the other 2 tablespoons of olive oil and sauté the shallots for two minutes on the top burner on medium-high heat.

Add the rack of lamb to the skillet and sear for two minutes per side until each section is seared. Turn the burner off and let sit for about five minutes.

With a pastry brush or your hands, rub the entire lamb with the Dijon mustard. Now roll it in the bread crumb mixture until the lamb is coated.

Grab some tinfoil and cover the ends of the bones to keep them from burning. Plus it totally looks cool.

Roast the lamb bone side down in the pre-heated oven for 12 to 18 minutes, Use a digital meat thermometer to ensure you cook it to your desired level of doneness. (See Tips below.)

Remove the lamb from the oven, cover loosely with tinfoil and allow to sit for ten minutes before carving.

Servings: 4

Dick's Difficulty Gauge: Moderately difficult

Oven Temperature: 450°F

Preparation Time: 20 minutes

Cooking Time: 20 minutes
Total Time: 40 minutes

Dicks Tips

Meat keeps cooking when you remove it from the oven Dick. This is why people will often over cook their meat when following the direction of the meat thermometer. To outsmart the thermometer remove any roast about 5 degrees short of the target doneness temperature. (I know 'doneness' isn't a word but it should be.) See Dicks Doneness Chart for cooking temperatures but you're likely shooting for a medium rare here Dick or 130° - 140° F.

One at a Time Ladies Lasagna

Beating them off with a stick Dick? I didn't think so. This lasagna however, will have them lined up and begging for more

1	tbsp	Olive oil
1	tbsp	Butter
1	med	Onion chopped
1½	lbs	Lean ground beef
3	cups	Six Month Mari-Me-Nara Sauce or alternate spaghetti sauce
1	can	Tomato Soup, condensed
2	large	Eggs, beaten
2	cups	Ricotta cheese
½	cup	Grated Parmesan cheese
1	pkg	Frozen chopped spinach, thawed and squeezed dry
1	box	Lasagna noodles - use the ready to bake variety that doesn't require pre-boiling to make things easier
3	cups	Shredded cheddar cheese
3	cups	Shredded mozzarella cheese

Procedure

In a large pot add olive oil and butter, melting over medium heat.

Add chopped onion and sauté for five minutes or until onion begins to soften.

Add lean ground beef and cook until no longer pink. If you need to, drain any excess fat from pan.

Add your Six Month Mari-Me-Mi-Nara Sauce and tomato soup to the pot and bring to a soft boil before reducing heat to simmer, stirring occasionally.

Preheat the oven to 350° F.

In a bowl mix together eggs, ricotta, parmesan and spinach.

Spray your 13" x 9" baking pan with non-stick cooking spray, and then pour 1 cup of the meat sauce in to cover the bottom of the pan.

Arrange 4 of your noodles in the bottom of the pan on top of the sauce.

Scoop out half of your cottage cheese mixture and spread over noodles. Cover that with about ¾ cup of the meat sauce and then top with a cup each of the shredded cheddar and mozzarella cheese.

Arrange 4 more noodles on top of that and repeat the above step, reserving some sauce for the top.

Finally place four more noodles on the top layer, pour remaining sauce over them and then sprinkle the remaining shredded cheese over top.

Cover the lasagna with tinfoil and bake in the oven for 30 minutes. Remove tinfoil and bake for an additional 5 - 10 minutes or until cheese is just starting to brown.

Remove from oven and allow to sit for 5 - 10 minutes prior to serving.

Servings: 8

Dick's Difficulty Gauge: Moderately difficult

Oven Temperature: 350°F

Preparation Time: 30 minutes
Cooking Time: 40 minutes
Inactive Time: 10 minutes
Total Time: 1 hour and 20 minutes

Dicks Tips

If you're not going to use the Six Month Mari-Me-Nara Sauce Dick (and really why wouldn't you?), then make sure you have a good sauce to use as a substitute. Kick it Italian style and serve up with some Dick's Bread and Butter garlic bread and Single and Sexy Caesar Salad.

Tap That Sea Bass

Ready to tap that? Set the mood first with this fantastic seafood dish that's simple and guaranteed to impress. Barring any aversion to fish that is.

4 Sea Bass fillets - 3/4 to 1 inch thickness	Crushed black peppercorns
½ cup Dick Likes It Creamy Caesar Salad Dressing	

Procedure

Spray a generous amount of non-stick cooking spray on the barbecue grill prior to lighting. Try to find the spray designed specifically for grilling and higher heat.

Fire up the barbecue to medium heat.

Rinse the sea bass fillets with cold water then pat dry with some paper towel.

Using a pastry brush, apply a generous amount of Dick Likes It Creamy Caesar Salad Dressing to the fillets.

With a pepper mill, coat both sides of the fish with crushed black pepper.

Grill for 6 to 8 minutes per side depending on how thick your fillets are. The center of the fish should be opaque and flaky.

Remove from grill and serve immediately.

Servings: 4
Yield: 4

Dick's Difficulty Gauge: Very easy

Preparation Time: 5 minutes
Cooking Time: 15 minutes
Total Time: 20 minutes

Dicks Tips

Sea bass is a little pricey Dick but well worth the investment. Three words will ensure a successful choice - fresh, fresh and fresh. Go straight to the seafood counter for this. Serve with Back in Black Bean Rice and Baked Tomato Tata's for a full meal.

Dick Factor: For presentation throw a sprig of dill on each fillet right before you serve it. For vino try a nice dry Riesling or a Chablis.

Throw Me a Bone Bake 'n Barbecue Ribs

These will be fall-off-the-bones delicious Dick and a great reason to brag about your meat. A great dish for any agenda and a perfect summer meal.

2 racks	Pork baby back ribs	1 tbsp	Garlic powder
¼ cup	Garlic flavored olive oil	1 tbsp	Montreal Steak Spice

Procedure

Preheat your oven to 200° F.

Line a baking sheet with tinfoil and spray evenly with cooking spray.

Cut your ribs into serving sized portions, or 3 - 4 rib pieces.

Place all pieces onto your baking sheet then brush both sides with the garlic flavoured olive oil.

Season both sides with garlic powder and steak spice.

Cover the top of the ribs with another sheet of tinfoil, tucking the sides in all around.

Bake in the oven at 200° F for about five hours.

When you're ready to eat, fire up the barbecue to a medium high heat.

Remove the ribs from the oven and brush with your favourite barbecue sauce before throwing on the barbecue. (If you prefer dry rub ribs just throw them directly on the barbecue minus the sauce.)

Grill for about 10 minutes, flipping once or twice and serve.

Servings: 6

Dick's Difficulty Gauge: Easy

Preparation Time: 30 minutes
Cooking Time: 5 hours and 15 minutes
Total Time: 5 hours and 45 minutes

Dicks Tips

Some Manly Macaroni Salad and some fresh cut veggies would go well with these ribs Dick. Have a small dish of warm water and lemon wedges for guests to clean their fingers. An empty dish on the table for the carcasses comes in handy as well.

MEET THE PARENTS

*"I like a cook who smiles out loud when he tastes his own work.
Let God worry about your modesty; I want to see your enthusiasm."
~ Robert Farrar Capon*

A Bow Tie Event

Can't afford a bow tie and tux, but still want to make a big impression? This dish looks awesome, tastes awesome and well, it's just awesome. So throw on some jeans, a comfy shirt and get ready to impress.

4	Boneless, skinless chicken breasts	1 tbsp	Basil Pesto
1 pkg	Bow Tie Pasta	4 lg	Tomatoes, seeded and chopped
¼ cup	Olive oil	½ cup	Parmesan cheese
3 cloves	Garlic, minced	¼ cup	Feta cheese
¼ cup	Pine nuts		

Procedure

Grill chicken breasts over the barbeque. Slice and set aside.

Cook pasta according to directions. Drain well then cover and set aside to keep warm.

In a small frying pan, heat olive oil over medium heat. Add garlic and sauté for five minutes, stirring frequently to avoid browning. Next add pine nuts, continuing to stir until nuts begin to tender, 5-7 minutes.

In a large bowl, toss pasta with olive oil mixture. Next add the basil and stir until all of the pasta is lightly coated.

Add remaining ingredients and stir together. Spread on a plate, and top with grilled chicken breast strips. Serve immediately.

Servings: 4

Dick's Difficulty Gauge: Easy

Preparation Time: 15 minutes
Cooking Time: 30 minutes
Total Time: 45 minutes

Dicks Tips

Pine nuts add a great, distinct flavour Dick and can be found at the grocery store in the baking section. This would serve well with Dick's Garlic Bread and some nice wine.

Penniless Beef Tenderloin

Be prepared to empty your wallet for a good cut of beef tenderloin Dick, but rest assured it will be money well spent. Cooked properly, this dish will be so tender it will melt in your mouth. Really, how could they not love you?

5	lbs	Beef Tenderloin roast	¼	cup	Balsamic vinegar
½	cup	Reduced sodium soy sauce	3		Garlic cloves, minced
¼	cup	Honey	1	tbsp	Coarse black pepper
1½	tbsp	Chopped ginger	3	tbsp	Cornstarch
½	cup	Dry red wine			

Procedure

In a glass pan large enough to hold the roast, mix all ingredients for the marinade together. Place the tenderloin in the dish and turn to coat. Cover with saran wrap and marinade overnight in the fridge, turning to coat every few hours.

Remove from fridge and warm to room temperature for about 4 hours prior to cooking.

Preheat oven to 400° F. Transfer tenderloin to a shallow baking pan, pouring marinade over top.

Cook for ten minutes at 400° F, and then reduce heat to 325° F for 40 more minutes for a medium rare roast. Baste with juices as roast cooks.

Remove from oven, cover or 'tent' with aluminum foil, and let stand for 10 minutes before serving.

Servings: 8

Dick's Difficulty Gauge: Easy

Oven Temperature: 325°F

Cooking Time: 50 minutes
Inactive Time: 12 hours
Total Time: 12 hours and 50 minutes

Dicks Tips

Make sure not to add any salt to your beef prior to cooking Dick, as this will toughen the meat. You'll find chopped ginger in small little jars in the produce department, along with the jarred garlic. Both are handy to have in the fridge.

Serve with Nearly Naked Garlic mashed potatoes and Asparadick and Hollandaise sauce for a truly elegant meal.

Bagger Steak with Béarnaise Sauce

A version of carpetbagger steak, this is sure to wow the pants of the parents, and oysters will help wow the pants off of her when they leave. Everybody feel the love.

3 tbsp	Butter	4 slices	Bacon, cooked and crumbled
1 cup	Fresh oysters, drained and chopped	1 ounce	Blue Cheese, crumbled
		½ cup	Dry white wine
½ cup	Mushrooms, chopped	4	Rib Eye Steaks
¼ cup	Shallots, finely chopped	1 pkg	Béarnaise Sauce
2 tsp	Fresh parsley, chopped		

Procedure

Leave steaks out to warm at room temperature for two hours before you plan to cook them.

In a fry pan over medium heat, melt butter and sauté oysters, mushrooms, shallots and parsley for about ten minutes, or until mushrooms are soft.

Drain off the excess butter and stir in the bacon, cheese, and wine. Continue cooking over medium-low heat for another ten minutes to slightly reduce the wine. Remove from heat and let cool for five minutes.

Meanwhile, make Béarnaise sauce according to package directions and simmer to keep warm.

Cut a pocket into the side of each steak then stuff pockets with the oyster mixture. Close the pocket as best you can, and secure with a wooden toothpick or two.

Grill steaks on the barbeque for about 6 minutes per side over high heat for medium doneness. If you are without barbecue Dick, you can broil the steaks about 6 inches from heat for about 8-10 minutes on each side.

Place steaks on serving plates and spoon any leftover mixture on top. Spoon Béarnaise sauce over steak and topping and serve.

Servings: 4

Dick's Difficulty Gauge: Moderately difficult

Preparation Time: 30 minutes

Cooking Time: 12 minutes
Inactive Time: 2 hours
Total Time: 2 hours and 42 minutes

Dicks Tips

You can pick up some fresh oysters at the fish counter Dick. These little pearls are said to be aphrodisiacs and should put everyone in the mood. Using the packaged Béarnaise sauce is time saving, simple and tastes just as good as stuff you'd make from scratch.

Crazy About Her Clam and Linguine

This simple delicious dish will let everyone know just how crazy you are about her... on the inside.

1 lb	Fresh linguine noodles	1 tsp	Red Pepper flakes, dried and crushed
1 tbsp	Olive oil		
1 tbsp	Butter	2 14½oz can	Diced tomatoes - Italian Seasoned one can drained of juices
1 med	Onion chopped		
2 tbsp	Garlic, minced	2 6oz can	Clams - chopped with juices reserved
1 tbsp	Anchovy paste		
		1 cup	Dry red wine (or white wine if you're stuck)
		¼ cup	Tomato paste

Procedure

Cook your linguine as directed on the package, then drain and set aside. Cover to keep warm.

Heat up your oil and butter in a large pot over medium-high heat, then add onion and sauté for 3 minutes or until they begin to soften. Stir frequently while they cook.

Now throw your garlic, anchovy paste and dried red pepper flakes into the mix, cooking for an additional 3 minutes.

Next you want to add your diced tomatoes. I want you to drain one can of all the liquids and add to the pot, then add the entire second can, liquids and all to the pot.

Now take the juice from your clams (the stuff I told you to keep Dick) and add to the pot. Don't add the actual clams just yet. Follow this with the red wine and tomato paste. Bring entire mixture to a soft boil for five minutes.

Now grab your clams and throw 'em in. Cook for 2 - 3 more minutes then remove from heat.

Take your cooked linguine noodles and add them to your sauce, tossing to coat.

Serve immediately with some Dicks Bread n' Butter, or crusty bread of your choice.

Servings: 4

Dick's Difficulty Gauge: Easy

Preparation Time: 10 minutes
Cooking Time: 30 minutes
Total Time: 40 minutes

Dicks Tips

Don't boil your sauce down too much Dick as this is supposed to be soupy and you don't want it to be too salty. You will likely find the anchovy paste with the canned seafood section where you find tuna, salmon and the like. If not, ask at the fish counter. You can also chop up 4 anchovy fillets to substitute for the paste.

French Guy Meat Pie

If you get caught with your finger in the pie Dick, this French-Canadian dish, better known as Tourtiere, will have them turning a blind eye to any indiscretions. A great choice for the holiday season as well.

1	tbsp	Olive oil
1	tbsp	Butter
3	sm	Sweet onions, finely chopped
2	lbs	Lean ground beef
1	lb	Lean ground pork
1½	cups	Beef broth or stock
4		Garlic cloves, crushed
1	tbsp	Salt
2	tsp	Pepper
1	tbsp	Herbes de Provence
½	tsp	Ground cloves
3	tsp	Cinnamon
1½	cups	Mashed potatoes
4		Frozen pie crusts - thawed at room temperature.
		Milk or cream

Procedure

In a large pot, melt olive oil and butter together over medium heat and sauté the onions for 5 - 7 minutes or until soft.

Add the ground beef and pork, and cook for 10 minutes or until no longer pink. Drain any excess fat out of the pot before the next steps.

Add the beef broth and remaining seasonings to the meat mixture and simmer on medium low until all the liquid has evaporated, for 20 - 30 minutes.

Remove from heat and stir in your mashed potatoes until thoroughly blended. Allow to cool in the refrigerator for 4 hours or more.

About a half hour before you're ready to bake, remove your frozen pie crusts and thaw on the counter at room temperature.

Preheat your oven to 350° F.

Once your crusts are soft, scoop the meat mixture evenly into two separate pie crusts, spreading evenly.

Gently remove the other two pie crusts from the tinfoil pan and lay on top of the filled meat mixture on both pies.

Gently pinch all around the edges of the crusts to seal them together.

Take a sharp knife and make a couple of slits into the top pie crusts to allow for steam to escape while baking. A few slices per pie will do it Dick.

Using your pastry brush, apply a thin coating of milk or cream on the top crust. Don't go crazy on this, just enough to moisten the shells.

Bake both pies in the center of the oven for 45 minutes. Remove and allow to cool for 10 minutes before serving.

Servings: 16
Yield: 2 Pies

Dick's Difficulty Gauge: Moderately difficult

Oven Temperature: 350°F

Preparation Time: 50 minutes
Cooking Time: 45 minutes
Inactive Time: 4 hours
Total Time:

Dicks Tips

This is a lot of pie Dick, but it's a lot of work and freezes well so we might as well make two. Eat one pie, freeze the other. Just slip it into an oversized Ziploc bag and throw it in the freezer. When you want to serve it, just thaw at room temperature or overnight in the fridge, then cover with foil and reheat in the oven at 350° F for 20 - 30 minutes or until heated through.

Fruit of Their Loins Grilled Halibut & Mango Salsa

Watch out Dick...this is their baby girl you're messing with. Use your boyish charm and this flavorful dish to win them over.

1 lg	Mango - peeled and finely chopped	1 tsp	Dried basil
1 med	Jalapeño pepper - seeded and finely chopped	¼ tsp	Salt
		2 tbsp	Olive oil
1 sm	Red onion - finely chopped	4 fillets	Halibut
2 tbsp	Lime juice	2 tbsp	Butter
2 tbsp	Chopped cilantro		

Procedure

Combine all the ingredients except the halibut and refrigerate until ready to use. Try to give this a good couple of hours to ensure all the flavours blend together.

In your nonstick skillet, heat 2 tablespoons of olive oil over medium high heat. Add the Halibut and sear for 5 minutes. Flip the fish over and add 2 tablespoons of butter. As the butter melts, spoon it over the Halibut and continue to cook for another 5 minutes.

Remove from the pan, arrange on your plates and spoon a generous portion of your Mango salsa on top. Serve immediately.

Servings: 4
Yield: 4

Dick's Difficulty Gauge: Very easy

Preparation Time: 10 minutes
Cooking Time: 10 minutes
Inactive Time: 2 hours
Total Time:

Dicks Tips

Halibut, like most white fish will dry out quickly if it's overcooked Dick. Cook only until the meat is no longer translucent and flakes easily. You can substitute pretty much any whitefish here.

Serve this up with some She's So Sweet Potato Frites and a fresh salad for a really healthy meal.

Gobble It Up Turkey Casserole

Any time's a good time for turkey, and this simple casserole dish will have them gobbling you up as well. Work it Dick, work it.

1¼ cups	Boiling water	½ cup	Milk
4 tbsp	Butter, melted	1 tsp	Garlic powder
4 cups	Dry stuffing mix	½ tsp	Thyme
2 cups	Cooked turkey, chopped	½ tsp	Sage
1 cup	Fresh or frozen broccoli	1 cup	Monterey Jack cheese, shredded
1 10oz can	Condensed Cream of Asparagus soup		

Procedure

Preheat oven to 350° F.

Bring water to a boil, remove from heat and stir in melted butter and stuffing mix. Spray the bottom of a 9" x13" inch pan or casserole dish with non-stick cooking spray, then layer the bottom of the pan with the stuffing mixture.

Evenly spread both the turkey and the broccoli over the stuffing mix.

In a separate bowl, mix together soup, milk, garlic, thyme, sage and half of the cheese.

Pour the mixture over the turkey and broccoli then sprinkle the rest of the cheese over top.

Bake uncovered for 30 minutes. Remove from oven and allow to sit for ten minutes before serving.

Servings: 6

Dick's Difficulty Gauge: Easy

Oven Temperature: 350°F

Preparation Time: 25 minutes
Cooking Time: 30 minutes
Inactive Time: 10 minutes
Total Time: 1 hour and 5 minutes

Dicks Tips

This is a great way to use up leftover turkey Dick, but you can always find cooked turkey breast at the grocery store as well, likely packaged up in the deli section. You can also throw pretty much any vegetable you'd like into this dish if you prefer something different.

I'm Really Not a Jackass Jambalaya

What better way to shake the Jackass handle than to prepare a fantastic southern dish that will look and taste like you spent hours in the kitchen? A great dish to impress the folks.

½ cup	Butter		3 cups	Frozen cooked shrimp
1 large	Spanish onion, finely chopped		2 28oz	Cans diced tomatoes
1 cup	Celery, chopped		1 6oz can	Tomato Paste
1 large	Green pepper, chopped		4 cups	Long-grain rice, uncooked
3	Garlic cloves, minced		3 tbsp	Cajun spice
7 cups	Chicken broth		2 tbsp	Hot sauce
3 cups	Oktoberfest Sausage, chopped		1 tbsp	Worcestershire sauce
3 cups	Chicken, cooked and chopped			

Procedure

Preheat the oven to 350° F.

In a large frying pan on medium heat, melt butter and sauté the onion, celery and green pepper for 10 minutes or until they begin to soften. Next add garlic and sauté for 2 minutes more then remove from heat.

In a large roasting pan combine all remaining ingredients, as well as sautéed vegetables. Stir thoroughly until all ingredients are combined.

Cover and bake for 1½ hours, stirring occasionally.

Servings: 10

Dick's Difficulty Gauge: Easy

Preparation Time: 30 minutes
Cooking Time: 1 hour and 30 minutes
Total Time: 2 hours

Dicks Tips

To save time later, you could throw this together early in the day and cook in a slow-cooker instead. Throw it in on high for about 4 hours or until the water is absorbed and the rice is cooked.

A Penne For Your Thoughts

In any good poker game you gotta be able to read the face of your opponents. Get them to relax with a big plate of pasta then try to read their thoughts while they sit and digest. Ante up!

1 pkg	Penne pasta		2 tbsp	Flour
2 tbsp	Butter		¾ cup	Chicken broth
1 tbsp	Olive oil		¾ cup	Milk or cream
1 cup	Mushrooms, chopped		1 tbsp	Parsley flakes
2 cloves	Garlic, minced		½ cup	Parmesan cheese
1 lb	Medium sized shrimp, cooked and peeled			Salt and pepper to taste

Procedure

Cook pasta according to package directions. Drain and cover to keep warm.

In a medium sized sauce pan over medium heat, melt butter and olive oil. Sauté mushrooms for ten minutes or until they begin to soften. Add garlic and continue to sauté for an additional five minutes.

Next, stir in shrimp and cook until heated through, for an additional five minutes.

Now add flour and cook for one minute, stirring constantly to blend with shrimp and mushrooms.

Next stir in broth and milk, stirring frequently until sauce boils and thickens.

Add parsley, parmesan cheese, salt and pepper and stir until cheese is melted.

In a large bowl, mix sauce with pasta and serve immediately.

Servings: 4

Dick's Difficulty Gauge: Easy

Preparation Time: 15 minutes
Cooking Time: 45 minutes
Total Time: 1 hour

Dicks Tips

It's important with any dish that involves heating milk, to stir the sauce continually so that it doesn't burn to the bottom of the pan. Make sure you've got everything to go as far as table settings and drinks, as this dish needs to be served right away before it cools.

Keeping it Wrapped Grilled Jumbo Shrimp

Wrapping it up is better for everyone Dick...and the parents will thank you for it.

½ cup	Raspberry jam	
½ cup	Sweet chili sauce	
12 large	Jumbo Shrimp	
¼ cup	Herbed Goat Cheese	
1 pkg	Cream cheese, room temperature	
1 tsp	Worcestershire sauce	
1 tsp	Garlic powder	
12 slices	Prosciutto - thinly sliced	

Procedure

Okay Dick, here we go. In a small bowl, combine your raspberry jam and sweet chili sauce. Refrigerate until ready to use.

Take your jumbo shrimp and peel the hard shell off, leaving the tail attached. Gently slice along the center belly of the shrimp to butterfly them, ensuring you don't cut them all the way through. Rinse and pat dry with a paper towel.

In a small mixing bowl, combine goat cheese, cream cheese, garlic and Worcestershire sauce until well blended.

Carefully spoon the cheese mixture into the pockets of the shrimp, filling each cavity.

Now take your prosciutto slices - and gently wrap each shrimp with one slice, ensuring to cover the pocket of cheese.

When you're ready to grill, fire up the barbecue to medium high.

If you have a barbecue cage, this is the easiest way to grill these. If not, try threading them onto skewers - three apiece.

Grill over medium high heat for about three minutes a side or until the shrimp meat is white.

Serve with the raspberry jam/sweet chili pepper sauce as a dip.

Servings: 4
Yield: 12

Dick's Difficulty Gauge: Easy

Preparation Time: 30 minutes

Cooking Time: 6 minutes
Total Time: 36 minutes

Dicks Tips

Look for some good sized shrimp here Dick so that your guests have enough to eat. Hit the seafood counter for something fresh. You could even substitute the shrimp for some nice prawns. If you're using the barbecue cage here (which I recommend) then spray it with some non-stick cooking spray before you put the shrimp in. If you grill directly on the barbecue, spray or oil that before you heat it up.

Meet the Chief Beef Stroganoff with Bacon

Including bacon in this recipe gives it a unique and flavorful taste. You're sure to impress the folks.

1 pkg	Egg Noodles, cooked according to package directions	2 tbsp	butter
½ lb	Bacon, chopped	½ cup	Spanish onion, chopped
3 tbsp	Butter	8oz	Sliced mushrooms
1 tbsp	Olive oil	¼ tsp	Nutmeg
2 lbs	Top sirloin steak, cut into 1 inch wide x 2 inch long strips	1 cup	Sour cream, room temperature
	Montreal Steak Spice to taste		Salt and pepper to taste

Procedure

Cook your Egg Noodles according to package directions. Strain in a colander and set aside. Leave the noodles in the colander for now.

In a small fry pan, cook bacon pieces until cooked but not crispy. Set aside in a medium sized bowl lined with a paper towel to soak up excess grease.

In a separate skillet, heat up olive oil and butter on medium-high heat. Add beef strips and fry for approximately four minutes, or just long enough to brown on both sides. Sprinkle with Montreal Steak Spice while frying. Remove strips from pan and set aside. (Throw the beef into the same bowl with the bacon, just remove the paper towel first.)

Using the same pan, add another 2 tbsp of butter and decrease your heat to medium. Toss in your onions and mushrooms, and sauté for five minutes.

Reduce the heat to low and cook for an additional two minutes. Next stir in the nutmeg and sour cream, ensuring to stir constantly. Don't allow the sour cream to boil Dick or it will curdle and screw up your sauce.

Once thoroughly mixed, add the bacon and beef strips to the pan and stir over low heat adding salt and pepper to your taste.

Rinse your noodles again with hot water to reheat them. Serve your stroganoff over the noodles.

Servings: 4

Dick's Difficulty Gauge: Easy

Preparation Time: 30 minutes
Cooking Time: 30 minutes
Total Time: 1 hour

Dicks Tips

If you can't find sirloin, ask the butcher for another tender cut of meat. Some Dicks Garlic Bread would be good on the side here too.

Their Little Lamb Chops

Mary had a little lamb, but Dick has got her now. And every time Dick makes this dish, his guests are surely wowed.

2 lbs	Lamb rib chops (2 ribs per chop Dick)	2 tsp	Coarse black pepper
2 tbsp	Fresh Rosemary, finely chopped	3	Garlic cloves, chopped or minced
2 tsp	Coarse sea salt	1 med	Lemon - halved

Procedure

Allow your lamb chops to sit out for an hour to bring them up to room temperature.

Meanwhile, back at the farm, mix the rosemary, salt, pepper, garlic, and 2 tablespoons of the olive oil together in a small dish until you get a well-blended paste.

Preheat the oven to 400° F. (This is only necessary if you want your lamb cooked more than rare.)

When you're ready to cook, squeeze some lemon juice onto your chops, then rub all over with the paste. (Don't apply the paste earlier Dick as the salt will draw out the moisture in your meat.)

In a large skillet, sear the lamb chops over medium high heat for about three minutes a side. If you're guests like it rare (which is the best way to serve lamb) then you're done. If they want the meat cooked a little more then remove your chops from the skillet, place on a baking sheet and bake in the oven for another five minutes.

Servings: 4

Dick's Difficulty Gauge: Easy

Oven Temperature: 400°F

Preparation Time: 10 minutes
Cooking Time: 6 minutes
Inactive Time: 1 hour
Total Time: 1 hour and 16 minutes

Dicks Tips

Try to find some nice thick chops for this one Dick. This is especially important if your guests like their meat cooked a little longer, so it doesn't dry out. Find yourself some nice mint jelly to go with this as well Dick.

Who's Your Daddy Chicken Diablo

Show her daddy whose boss in the kitchen with this fantastic chicken dish. Show her who her real daddy is when he leaves.

4	Boneless, skinless chicken breasts	¼ tsp	Paprika
½ cup	Sour cream	¼ tsp	Cumin
¼ cup	Frank's Hot Sauce	2 tbsp	Olive oil
¼ cup	Ketchup	2	Garlic cloves, minced
2 tbsp	Honey		

Procedure

Using your meat tenderizer, beat chicken breasts to one third their original thickness.

In a shallow glass baking dish, mix together sour cream, hot sauce, ketchup, honey, paprika and cumin. Set aside half of the marinade in another dish. In the baking dish place the chicken breasts in the remaining sauce, coating completely, and refrigerate for three hours or more.

Heat olive oil in a large frying pan over medium heat and sauté garlic for two minutes. Take your marinated breasts and pan fry in the olive oil on medium high on both sides until lightly browned, or about 10 minutes per side.

In a small sauce pot, bring marinade to a boil then reduce heat and simmer for five minutes.

Serve chicken with drizzled marinade over top.

Servings: 4

Dick's Difficulty Gauge: Easy

Preparation Time: 10 minutes
Cooking Time: 25 minutes
Inactive Time: 3 hours
Total Time: 3 hours and 20 minutes

Dicks Tips

All you need to finish this off Dick is a batch of white instant rice to serve under the chicken and a side salad. Oh, and maybe a pitcher of ice water.

Three Sheets to the Wind Chicken

Whatever you do, don't engage in nervous drinking before the parents arrive or you too will be three sheets to the wind. Focus instead on pulling off this challenging but fantastic dish.

4 lg	Boneless, skinless chicken breasts	12 sheets	Phyllo Pastry (you may want to have a few extras for backup Dick)
1 pkg	Brie cheese, shredded		
¼ cup	Cranberry sauce		
½ cup	Butter, melted		

Procedure

Okay Dick, this recipe will challenge you just a little but I have faith in you. Let's start by combining your shredded brie and cranberry sauce in a small bowl to prepare the filling.

Now preheat your oven to 350° F.

Your next step is to carefully cut a lengthwise pocket into the thickest part of the chicken breast so you have enough space for the filling. Don't cut the chicken all the way through - make sure it stays intact.

Spoon a quarter of the mixture into each pocket being careful not to over stuff it. You should be good with about 2 - 3 tablespoons depending on the size of the breasts.

Place the first sheet of phyllo on your working surface, keeping the rest covered with a damp paper towel to keep it from drying out. Gentle Dick - this tears easily.

Using your pastry brush, gently brush the first phyllo sheet with the melted butter. Put the second sheet on top and brush with butter. Finish with the third sheet and again brush with butter.

Now place your stuffed chicken breast near the bottom center of the short edge of the pastry. Leave a couple of inches from the bottom.

Carefully roll the chicken up, tucking in the sides as you go.

Now place the rolled up chicken seam side down on a large baking sheet sprayed with non-stick cooking spray.

Brush the tops with a little more butter and bake in the oven for 45 minutes.

Remove from the oven, puff your chest out victoriously and serve.

Servings: 4

Dick's Difficulty Gauge: Moderately difficult

Oven Temperature: 350°F

Dicks Tips

You will find phyllo pastry in the frozen food section Dick. Make sure you read the package directions and allow ample time for the pastry to thaw before using it. It's very thin so handle with care.

What a Ham

Time for Dick to be the center of attention. This is an easy baked ham recipe that will have all eyes on you tonight.

10 lbs Smoked ham - bone in	½ cup Whole grain Dijon mustard
1 cup Water	½ cup Brown sugar, packed
1 cup Apple cider, or apple juice	2 tbsp Butter
1 cup Honey	

Procedure

Warm up the oven to 325° F.

Place your ham in a large roasting pan, using a drip rack if you've got one. Add one cup of water to the bottom of the pan, then pour the apple juice over the ham.

Cover the roasting pan with a lid or aluminum foil and bake in the oven for 3½ hours.

Meanwhile, combine the honey, Dijon mustard and brown sugar in a small sauce pan. Cook over medium-low heat, stirring occasionally for 3 - 5 minutes or until all ingredients are dissolved and blended. Remove from heat and allow to sit - we'll use this glaze later Dick.

When your ham is done remove from the oven and bump up the temperature to 400° F.

Using a sharp knife 'score' a shallow 1" diamond pattern all over the entire ham. You can do this Dick. (See Tips.)

Now, using your pastry brush, baste the ham with half of your glaze mixture and return uncovered to the oven.

Continue to bake for another 30 - 40 minutes, basting with the glaze until it's all used up and you have a nice golden crust on the ham.

Remove from the oven and allow to sit for at least 20 minutes before you carve that baby up.

Servings: 10

Dick's Difficulty Gauge: Moderately difficult

Oven Temperature: 325°F

Preparation Time: 15 minutes
Cooking Time: 4 hours
Inactive Time: 20 minutes
Total Time:

Dicks Tips

What the hell does it mean to score the meat? It's a nice fancy cooking word for making shallow cuts in a roast, usually in a diamond shaped pattern. This serves two purposes; First and foremost it looks awesome Dick. Secondly, it creates a tender cut of meat and allows for excess fat to drip away. See? You learned something today Dick.

Serve this up with some Gold Digger Scalloped Potatoes, along with some Ears Like Cauliflower Casserole for a full menu. (You can make these ahead of time then reheat in the oven while the ham sits.)

Three Months' Salary My Ass Salmon

This is one of the easiest recipes in the book Dick. Fresh salmon, a barbecue and a smile is all you need to pull this off.

1	Cedar Plank - soaked in water for 30 minutes or more	½ cup	Sweet chili sauce (or enough to cover the entire top portion of the salmon)
2 lbs	Atlantic salmon		

Procedure

Grab your salmon and give it a good rinse under cold water to make sure it's as fresh as possible, then pat dry with a paper towel.

Lay the salmon on top of your cedar plank.

Spread the sweet chili sauce over top of the salmon.

Heat the barbecue up to medium heat. When you're ready to grill, turn either the center burner off (for a three burner barbecue) or one of the sides. Place the cedar plank with salmon over top of the portion of the barbecue grill that has no direct heat.

Cook for about 30 minutes or until the fish is a light pink and easily flakes. Don't overcook the fish or you'll dry it out.

Remove from heat and serve immediately.

Servings: 4

Dick's Difficulty Gauge: Very easy

Preparation Time: 5 minutes
Cooking Time: 35 minutes
Total Time: 40 minutes

Dicks Tips

Repeat after me Dick...I will buy fresh fish. Also, if you don't have a cedar plank handy, you can cook this on some heavy duty tin foil as well. Just place the salmon on a sheet of foil, bend the sides up but keep the top open.

OFF SIDE

"The meal is not over when I'm full. The meal is over when I hate myself." ~ *Louis C.K.*

Asparadick and Hollandaise

Asparagus takes three years to harvest Dick. You however, should be able to pull this recipe off in less than 20 minutes. You can also use this sauce for salmon, chicken, veggies or eggs benedict.

1	bunch	Asparagus	2 tbsp	Lemon juice
3		Egg yolks	1 tbsp	Hot water
½ cup		Melted butter	1 dash	Cayenne pepper

Procedure

Wash and de-stalk the asparagus. This is easily done by simply bending the asparagus in half, and it will snap in the right spot. Discard the stems.

Place asparagus in a microwavable dish, and pour about a half inch of water at the bottom. Cover, and microwave on high for three minutes or until desired firmness is reached.

In a small sauce pan, lightly beat the egg yolks. Add the remaining ingredients and stirring constantly, heat over low heat until sauce reaches a thick consistency.

Strain water from asparagus dish and cover with hollandaise. Serve right away.

Servings: 4

Dick's Difficulty Gauge: Easy

Preparation Time: 5 minutes
Cooking Time: 15 minutes
Total Time: 20 minutes

Dicks Tips

Separate the egg white from the yolk by cracking the egg in half, and then over the sink, transfer the yolk back and forth from shell to shell allowing the egg white to fall into the sink. Be sure to get rid of as much white as you can or your sauce will be runny.

If you want to be a frugal Dick, keep the leftover stems and use them to make Stalker Soup.

Back in Black Bean Rice

This recipe is a great side dish, and easy to prepare. The turmeric will not only give your rice a nice flavor, but according to recent studies, it's also beneficial in fighting and preventing prostate cancer! This allows you to take care of your belly and your boys.

2 cups	White rice, cooked as per directions	¼ cup	Red peppers, chopped
½ tbsp	Dried oregano	¼ cup	Green peppers, chopped
¼ tsp	Turmeric spice	2 cloves	Garlic, minced
1 tbsp	Olive oil	1 15oz can	Black beans, rinsed and drained
1 tbsp	Butter	3 dashes	Tabasco or hot sauce
½ cup	Cooking onions, chopped		Salt and pepper to taste

Procedure

Cook white rice as per package directions. Stir in oregano and turmeric then set aside, leaving covered to retain heat.

In a medium sized skillet, melt butter with the olive oil over medium heat. Sauté onions, peppers and garlic for about ten minutes, or until soft.

Stir in beans and hot sauce. Reduce heat to medium-low and heat through bean mixture for five minutes.

Mix the beans and the rice together, seasoning with salt and pepper to taste. Place in a casserole or serving dish and keep covered until ready to serve.

Servings: 6

Dick's Difficulty Gauge: Easy

Preparation Time: 10 minutes
Cooking Time: 30 minutes
Total Time: 40 minutes

Dicks Tips

Instant rice is easiest here Dick. Pretty much fool-proof and guaranteed to be fluffy. As for the turmeric, you can find this spice along with all the others at the grocery store. Most spices are stocked in alphabetical order.

Baked Tomato Tata's

A great side dish to serve with chicken or fish. Simple to prepare and the presentation is great.

2 tbsp	Garlic flavored olive oil	1 tsp	Coarse salt
2 pints	Roma tomatoes	1 tsp	Coarse black pepper
¼ cup	Fresh basil, chopped	¼ cup	Parmesan cheese, freshly grated or thinly sliced

Procedure

Preheat oven to 400° F.

In a baking dish, toss together olive oil, tomatoes, salt and pepper. Bake for ten minutes or until tomatoes begin to plump, but make sure they don't split open.

Sprinkle freshly grated parmesan cheese over the tomatoes and bake for an additional 2 minutes or until cheese melts.

Servings: 4

Dick's Difficulty Gauge: Very easy

Dicks Tips

Fresh parmesan cheese is essential here Dick...don't be tempted to substitute with the grated parmesan in the fridge. You can pick up a small brick or container of freshly shredded parmesan cheese at the deli counter in the grocery store. Failing that, go for some thinly sliced mozzarella.

Bare Naked Garlic Mashed Potatoes

An all-time classic if done properly, mashed potatoes are the perfect side kick to a great meal.

4 lbs	Yukon Gold Potatoes, peeled and cubed	¼ cup	Butter
2 tbsp	Coarse sea salt	6 cloves	Garlic, minced
1½ cups	Half and half cream	½ cup	Havarti cheese, grated

Procedure

In a large pot of water, add your potatoes and salt and bring to a rolling boil. Cook until the potatoes are soft and flake apart easily. This should take 20 minutes or so Dick, depending on how big your potato cubes are.

Remove from heat, strain and return potatoes to the pot.

Meanwhile, in a small sauce pan heat your cream, butter and garlic on medium low for 3 - 4 minutes or until well blended.

Pour your heated cream into pot and either mash or blend with an electric mixer until smooth.

Now add your grated cheese and mix/mash further until melted and well blended. Serve immediately.

Servings: 6

Dick's Difficulty Gauge: Easy

Preparation Time: 15 minutes
Cooking Time: 20 minutes
Total Time: 35 minutes

Dicks Tips

You could always garnish these potatoes with a couple of tablespoons of finely chopped fresh chives. Adds a nice flavour and ups the presentation.

Bitchin' Broccoli Salad

Nobody will bitch about this dish Dick. Healthy, full of flavour and great with any summer meal.

¾ cups	Mayonnaise	2	heads	Broccoli
¼ cup	Sugar	1	cup	Red grapes, washed and cut in half
1 tbsp	Lemon juice			
1 tbsp	Worcestershire sauce	1	bunch	Green onions
½ cup	Cooked, crumbled bacon	1½ cups		Shredded cheddar cheese, old

Procedure

In a medium sized bowl, mix the mayonnaise, sugar, lemon juice and Worcestershire sauce. Refrigerate and allow to sit for at least 30 minutes.

Cook bacon (about 10 slices) until crisp. Drain fat, cool and chop.

Wash and chop broccoli, grapes and onions. Pat dry and combine in a large bowl. Add bacon and shredded cheese.

Mix in dressing and thoroughly coat the entire salad. Refrigerate until ready to eat.

Servings: 8

Dick's Difficulty Gauge: Easy

Preparation Time: 30 minutes
Cooking Time:
Total Time: 30 minutes

Dicks Tips

Again Dick, mayo is a must. Do not succumb to any substitute or you're dressing will be too sweet. This can be made early in the day as long as it's kept refrigerated.
Dick Factor: For a twist on the recipe, try mixing in a package of Onion Soup Mix into the sauce but give yourself at least an hour for the soup mix to soften. Also, sprinkling the top with some sunflower seeds as a nice touch.

Corn off the Wagon

Easy summer side dish with a healthy dose of manliness. "Sex is good, but not as good as fresh sweet corn." ~ Garrison Keillor

1 cup Butter	1 tbsp Sugar
1 can Beer	Water - enough to cover corn
1 tbsp Salt	8 Cobs of Corn

Procedure

In a large pot, add your butter, beer, salt, sugar and water and turn stove on high to bring to a boil.

Husk all of your corn and place in pot, boiling for about 15 minutes or until corn is tender.

Servings: 8

Dick's Difficulty Gauge: Very easy

Dicks Tips

All corn is not created equal Dick. When picking it out at the grocery store, pull the top part of the husk back to ensure you've got yourself a good cob. Look for bright coloured corn that's healthy to the tip. Peaches and Cream corn is probably your best choice if you can find it.

Carb-a-Palooza Potato Casserole

Not for the calorie or carb conscious Dick, but for everyone else it's game on. This casserole dish is awesome.

- 1 pkg Stuffing mix
- 4 lbs Potatoes, peeled and cut into cubes
- 1 cup Cream
- ½ cup Butter
- 1 tsp Garlic powder (not salt Dick, powder)
- 1 tsp Salt
- 1 tsp Black pepper
- 1 cup Mozzarella cheese, shredded
- ¾ cup Parmesan cheese
- ½ cup Gruyere cheese, shredded

Procedure

Cook stuffing mixture according to package directions and set aside.

Preheat your oven to 350° F.

In a large pot boil potatoes in salted water for 10 - 15 minutes or until soft. Drain and return the potatoes to the pot.

Add your cream, butter, garlic, salt and pepper and mash well, making sure there's no lumps Dick.

Now mix in your cheese until well blended then spoon into a casserole or baking dish that has been coated with non-stick cooking spray.

Spread the stuffing mixture evenly across the top of the potatoes and bake for 30 minutes.

Remove and serve.

Servings: 6

Dick's Difficulty Gauge: Easy

Oven Temperature: 350°F

Preparation Time: 30 minutes
Cooking Time: 30 minutes
Total Time: 1 hour

Dicks Tips

To add a little Dude to your casserole, throw in a pound of cooked and chopped bacon into the potato mixture.

Dick's Own Barbecue Salad

Who says you can't make a salad on the barbecue? That's right Dick...a barbecued salad.

4 cups	Spring mix salad	3	Garlic cloves, minced
2 large	Portabella mushrooms, stem removed, washed and chopped	1 cup	Newman's Own Balsamic Vinaigrette Dressing
1 med	Red pepper, seeded and chopped into bite sized pieces	1 cup	Cherry tomatoes halved
		½ cup	Feta cheese crumbled
1 med	Green pepper, seeded and chopped into bite sized pieces		
1 med	Red Onion, chopped into bite sized pieces		

Procedure

Divide the spring mix evenly onto four salad plates.

Using a tinfoil barbecue pan, add the mushrooms, peppers, onion, garlic and Balsamic Vinaigrette dressing, stirring to coat. Cover with tinfoil.

Place on the barbecue and grill over medium high heat for 15 minutes, stirring occasionally to coat. The dressing will boil and the veggies will start to soften.

Add the cherry tomatoes and continue to cook for another 5 minutes.

Remove from heat and spoon directly over the spring mix salad, ensuring to include some of the salad dressing.

Sprinkle salads with crumbled feta and serve immediately.

Servings: 4

Dick's Difficulty Gauge: Easy

Dicks Tips

You don't want to add the tomatoes too soon Dick or you'll end up with little mush balls. Cook your veggies to taste but make sure they maintain a little bit of crunch. You can also substitute freshly shaved parmesan cheese for the feta if you prefer.

Dirty Girl Rice

Many versions of this recipe are made with chicken giblets and livers. Here's one made with ground beef instead. I'm sure you can find another use for organ meat elsewhere Dick.

4 cups	Long-grain rice, cooked		½ tsp	Celery salt
1 lb	Lean ground beef		1 tbsp	Cajun seasoning
½ cup	Red peppers, chopped		½ cup	Water
½ cup	Green onions, chopped			Salt and pepper to taste
½ tsp	Garlic powder			

Procedure

Cook rice according to package directions. Cover to keep warm and set aside.

In a large frying pan over medium-high heat, cook together the ground beef and red peppers just until beef is no longer pink. Be sure to break up ground beef as much as possible. Drain excess fat if necessary.

Turn heat down to medium-low and add rice and remaining ingredients, stirring well to combine. Cook for 30 minutes or until all of the water is absorbed. Season with salt and pepper to suit your taste.

Remove from heat and let sit uncovered for five minutes before serving.

Servings: 6

Dick's Difficulty Gauge: Easy

Preparation Time: 10 minutes
Cooking Time: 40 minutes
Total Time: 50 minutes

Dicks Tips

This serves as a great side dish with Cold Shoulder, Hot Catfish.

Ears Like Cauliflower Casserole

The sharp cheddar cheese in this recipe really throws a punch. Bob and weave Dick, bob and weave.

1	large	Head of cauliflower - rinsed and cut into bite sized pieces	½ pkg	Cream cheese, room temperature
1	tbsp	Coarse sea salt	1½ cups	Sharp cheddar cheese, grated
2	tbsp	Butter	¼ cup	Parmesan cheese
2	med	Shallots, chopped	¾ cup	Italian Style seasoned breadcrumbs
½	cup	Half and half cream		

Procedure

Bring a large pot of salted water to a boil and cook cauliflower pieces for 6 minutes or until slightly tender then strain.

Preheat the oven to 350° F.

Spray a baking dish with non-stick cooking spray and place the strained cauliflower pieces in the dish.

In a separate sauce pan, melt the butter over medium heat and sauté shallots for three minutes or until tender.

Now using the same sauce pan add the cream, cream cheese and one cup of the shredded cheese. Stir constantly over medium heat for five minutes or until the cheese is melted and well blended.

Now pour your cheese sauce over the cauliflower.

Combine your bread crumbs and parmesan cheese together in a small bowl and spread over the top of the cauliflower. Top with remaining shredded cheese and bake for 25 minutes.

Remove from heat and allow to sit for 5 minutes before serving.

Servings: 4

Dick's Difficulty Gauge: Moderately difficult

Oven Temperature: 350°F

Preparation Time: 20 minutes

Cooking Time: 25 minutes
Inactive Time: 5 minutes
Total Time: 50 minutes

Dicks Tips

You can add some variety to this dish Dick by substituting half of your cauliflower for some broccoli.

"Cauliflower is nothing but cabbage without a college education." ~ Mark Twain

Gold Digger Scalloped Potatoes

This may be considered culinary cheating Dick, but if she's indeed a gold-digger then you're judgment free.

5 large	Yukon Gold Potatoes	1½ cups	Milk
1 med	Red onion	¼ cup	Butter, melted
1 10oz	Can Campbell's Condensed Cream of Mushroom and Garlic soup		Paprika

Procedure

Preheat the oven to 375° F.

Wash and peel potatoes then thinly slice. (A little thicker than a potato chip).

Chop red onion into small pieces.

In a bowl, combine soup mixture and milk. Stir until well blended.

Spray a large casserole dish with non-stick cooking spray. Next, layer a third each of the potatoes, onion, butter and soup mix. Sprinkle lightly with paprika. Repeat two more times until all ingredients are in the dish.

Bake uncovered for 1 hour 45 minutes, or until potatoes are tender.

Servings: 6

Dick's Difficulty Gauge: Easy

Oven Temperature: 375°F

Preparation Time: 15 minutes
Cooking Time: 1 hour and 45 minutes
Total Time: 2 hours

Dicks Tips

Regular cream of mushroom soup will do here as well if you can't find the type with garlic or don't like garlic. Also, if you'd like to cut down some of the baking time, microwave potato slices first for about 10 minutes to give them a head start.

The Dick Factor: If you're the king of cheese Dick, sprinkle one cup of grated cheddar over top of the casserole about 40 minutes into baking it and garnish with some parsley.

Manly Macaroni Salad

A great summer side dish with anything barbecued - especially with some I'm The Man Hamburgers.

3	cups	Rotini Vegetable Pasta	2 tsp	Celery salt
¼	cup	Red onion, chopped	2 tsp	Seasoned Salt
¼	cup	Green Onions, chopped	2 tsp	Pepper
1	can	Tuna, packed in water	½ cup	Mayonnaise
2	tsp	Dried dill		

Procedure

In a large sauce pan, boil pasta in about 8 cups of water, or according to package directions.

Meanwhile, chop onions and drain tuna.

Once pasta has reached desired consistency, drain using a strainer and rinse with cold water.

In a large bowl, mix together all the ingredients. Transfer to a smaller serving bowl and refrigerate for at least two hours before serving. Depending on personal taste, you may want to add more mayonnaise prior to serving.

Servings: 6

Dick's Difficulty Gauge: Easy

Preparation Time: 30 minutes
Cooking Time:
Inactive Time: 1 hour and 30 minutes
Total Time: 2 hours

Dicks Tips

Mayonnaise is a must here Dick. Don't be tempted to buy Miracle Whip or 'Mayonnaise Type' dressings as they will be sweeter in taste. And yes, there is a difference between the two.

The Dick Factor: Don't use plain old macaroni noodles - dull dull dull. The vegetable or tri-colored Rotini really ups the presentation.

Nice Yams

"I yam what I yam, and that's all that I yam." - Popeye the Sailor Man.

4 large	Yams or sweet potatoes, peeled	½ cup	Grated Parmesan cheese
½ cup	Dick's Garlic Butter		Season Salt to taste

Procedure

Peel your yams and pierce all over with a fork.

Place the yams on a plate and microwave on high for 6 minutes then reposition on the plate and microwave for an additional 6 minutes. They should be soft but firm enough to hold their shape when sliced.

Allow to cool slightly so you can handle them, then slice lengthwise into 1" thick pieces.

Using your pastry brush, coat both sides of the yams with garlic butter. It should melt into the yams as they will still be warm.

Next sprinkle both sides with parmesan cheese and lightly season with seasoned salt.

Grill directly on the barbecue over medium heat for 3 - 5 minutes per side, allowing for cool grill marks.

Serve immediately.

Servings: 4

Dick's Difficulty Gauge: Very easy

Preparation Time: 20 minutes
Cooking Time: 10 minutes
Total Time: 30 minutes

Dicks Tips

The only trick here Dick is gauging how long to microwave the yams. They can't be too soft as they'll fall apart, but they're only grilled long enough to sear in the garlic butter and seasoning. Just check them by piercing with a knife to determine firmness. Think of a firm baked potato.

Pre-Nup Fried Zucchini

Sign here. Pass the zucchini.

½ cup	Italian Style seasoned breadcrumbs		1 tsp	Salt
½ cup	Grated parmesan cheese		1 tsp	Black pepper
2 tsp	Garlic powder		4 lg	Zucchini - peeled and sliced into quarters
1 tsp	Herbes de Provence seasoning		2 lg	Eggs, beaten
1 tsp	Red pepper flakes		1 cup	Vegetable oil

Procedure

In a shallow dish combine all the seasoning thoroughly to combine.

Dip each zucchini stick in the egg mixture then coat with bread crumb mixture. Arrange on a paper towel until they are all coated and ready to go.

In a large frying pan, heat up vegetable oil over medium heat. Add the zucchini sticks and pan fry until golden brown, flipping over occasionally to ensure even browning. This shouldn't take much more than 3 minutes Dick.

Remove from the pan and place back onto the paper towel to absorb any excess oil. Serve immediately or cover to keep warm until you're ready for them.

Servings: 4

Dick's Difficulty Gauge: Easy

Preparation Time: 10 minutes
Cooking Time: 3 minutes
Total Time: 13 minutes

Dicks Tips

These are great as a side vegetable or an appetizer Dick. If serving as an app, throw in some ranch dressing or Dick's Tzatziki Sauce for a dip. Awesome.

Seeing Red Potato Salad

Something have you seeing red Dick? This chilled potato salad will cool you off and fill you up.

1 cup	Mayonnaise	
½ cup	Sour cream	
1 tsp	Dijon mustard	
1 tsp	Celery salt	
1 tsp	Dried dill	

5 lbs	Red potatoes - peeled and halved
6 large	Eggs, hard boiled and peeled
½ cup	Red onion, finely chopped
4 stalks	Celery, chopped
4 med	Radish, chopped

Procedure

- In a small bowl, combine mayo, sour cream, Dijon mustard, celery salt and dill. Mix thoroughly and refrigerate until ready to use
- In a large pot, boil your potatoes for about 10 minutes or until slightly soft. You don't want them to be mushy and break apart Dick, but you don't want them too firm either.
- Once cooked, drain and allow to sit in cold water for another ten minutes or so to cool them off.
- Cut the potatoes into bite sized pieces and place in a large bowl.
- Chop your hard boiled eggs into small pieces and add them to the bowl, followed with your chopped veggies.
- Slowly add your mayo/sour cream mixture a little at a time until you reach your desired consistency, ensuring to evenly coat all the potatoes.
- Refrigerate for an hour or longer prior to serving. You can add more of the mayo mixture as it chills as some may be absorbed by the potatoes.

Servings: 8

Dick's Difficulty Gauge: Easy

Preparation Time: 45 minutes
Cooking Time:
Inactive Time: 1 hour

Total Time:

Dicks Tips

You can add more seasoning to this Dick to adjust to your own personal taste. If you run out of the mayo/sour cream mixture just use straight mayo to top it up.

She's So Sweet Potato Frites

Sweet potatoes for a sweet date Dick.

4 med	Sweet potatoes		½ tsp	Season Salt
¼ cup	Olive oil		½ tsp	Nutmeg
1 tbsp	Mrs. Dash Extra Spicy seasoning		½ tsp	Garlic powder
½ tbsp	Coarse sea salt			

Procedure

Preheat oven to 425° F.

Wash sweet potatoes, but do not peel. Slice into French fry sized pieces.

In a large bowl, combine all ingredients and toss to coat. Spread evenly on a cookie sheet and place in oven. Bake for 60 minutes, turning over half way through.

Servings: 4

Dick's Difficulty Gauge: Very easy

Oven Temperature: 425°F

Preparation Time: 10 minutes
Cooking Time: 1 hour
Total Time: 1 hour and 10 minutes

Dicks Tips

Find some good sized sweet potatoes (also called yams) for this recipe Dick, simply for ease of handling when you slice them up. If you want to save some cooking time, you could microwave the sliced pieces for five minutes or so, then throw them in the oven.

You could also serve these with a small side of Dick's Tzatziki Sauce for dipping.

Teaser Tomato and Cucumber Salad

Got yourself a tease? Give her a taste of her own medicine along with this teaser of a dish.

3 med	Tomatoes, sliced	¼ cup	Olive oil
2 med	Cucumbers, peeled and sliced	¼ cup	Vinegar
1 med	Sweet onion, thinly sliced	1 tsp	Basil
	Montreal Steak Spice to taste		

Procedure

Layer veggies in a bowl, lightly sprinkling the Montreal Steak Spice between each layer.

In a separate bowl, combine remaining ingredients and mix. Pour contents over the vegetables and refrigerate for one hour.

Servings: 4

Dick's Difficulty Gauge: Very easy

Preparation Time: 15 minutes
Cooking Time:
Inactive Time: 1 hour
Total Time: 1 hour and 15 minutes

Dicks Tips

Fresh veggies are the only secret here Dick. If you want to spruce it up, sprinkle some Herbes de Provence seasoning on the top of the dish before serving.

Rice Peel-Off

Peel off a layer or two with this South Asian inspired staple.

¼ cup	Butter	1 cup	Regular long-grain rice, uncooked
1 lg	Spanish onion, thinly sliced	¼ tsp	Thyme
1 cup	Fresh mushrooms, sliced	2 cups	Chicken broth
½ cup	Yellow peppers, chopped		

Procedure

Preheat oven to 350° F.

In a frying pan melt half the butter over medium heat and sauté the onion, green peppers and mushrooms for about ten minutes or until soft. Set aside in a bowl.

Using the same pan, melt the remaining butter over medium heat and add your rice. Stir frequently until slightly browned, or about 5 minutes.

Next pour in the chicken broth and stir for three minutes. Pour the rice mixture and sautéed vegetables into a medium sized casserole dish. Cover and bake for 40 minutes or until liquid is completely absorbed and rice is fluffy.

Servings: 4

Dick's Difficulty Gauge: Easy

Oven Temperature: 350°F

Preparation Time: 20 minutes
Cooking Time: 40 minutes
Total Time: 1 hour

Dicks Tips

This is a simple side dish and serves well alongside fish or chicken.

Wicked Wedges

These serve well on their own as a side dish, or make as a munchie and serve with some Dicks Sour Cream for dipping.

5 lg	Potatoes, washed but not peeled	1 tbsp	Balsamic vinegar
2 tbsp	Cajun spice	1 tsp	Cayenne pepper
1 tbsp	Ground cumin	¼ cup	Olive oil
1 tbsp	Ground coriander		

Procedure

Preheat oven to 400° F.

Scrub the potatoes and cut each into six wedges.

In a large bowl, combine the potatoes, seasoning and olive oil. Mix well to coat the wedges.

Lay out the wedges on a baking sheet and bake in the oven for 40 minutes. Flip them over for another 20 minutes or until crisp.

Servings: 4
Yield: 30

Dick's Difficulty Gauge: Easy

Oven Temperature: 400°F

Preparation Time: 15 minutes
Cooking Time: 1 hour
Total Time: 1 hour and 15 minutes

Dicks Tips

When choosing a potato, the P.E.I. washed potatoes with the thin skin are a good choice.

Wine and Cheese Biscuits

Looking for a little cheese with that whine? Light and flaky, these biscuits are fantastic and go well with most any main dish Dick.

2½ cups	Bisquick baking mix		½ tsp	Dried parsley
1 cup	Cheddar cheese, finely grated		¼ cup	Dicks Garlic Butter, melted
¾ cup	White wine			

Procedure

Preheat oven to 400° F.

In a large bowl, combine all ingredients except for the garlic butter. Mix until well combined.

Drop approximately ¼ cup portions into an un-greased muffin pan or onto an un-greased cookie sheet.

Brush with Dicks Garlic Butter then bake for 15 minutes, or until the muffins begin to brown.

Serve warm, brushing with more garlic butter when you remove them from the oven.

Servings: 6
Yield: 12

Dick's Difficulty Gauge: Easy

Oven Temperature: 400°F

Preparation Time: 15 minutes
Cooking Time: 15 minutes
Total Time: 30 minutes

Dicks Tips

You can find Bisquick baking mix in the same area as you would pancake mix Dick. It's a handy staple to have around as it serves many uses.

If you're fresh out of wine (which of course should never happen) you can substitute with milk. These are best served warm so be sure to fire them on the table as soon as you take them out of the oven. After dinner, go to the liquor store and get more wine.

Email the author at:

seedickcook@hotmail.com

Index

A
A Bow Tie Event 162
A Penne For Your Thoughts 178
A Swing And A Miss Chipotle Chicken 83
A Total Cheese Ball 31
Asparadick and Hollandaise 194

B
Bachelor Bites 32
Back in Black Bean Rice 196
Bad Boy Bruschetta 34
Bagger Steak with Bearnaise Sauce 166
Baked Tomato Tata's 198
Banger and Dash 76
Bare Naked Garlic Mashed Potatoes 199
Beer Me Cheddar Soup 102
Big Balls Spaghetti 132
Bitchin' Broccoli Salad 200
Bite Me Sheppard's Pie 78
Blackened Sole 80
Bombshell Burrito's 134

C
Carb-a-Palooza Potato Casserole 202
Chili on a Bender 104
Ciao Bella Steak 106
Cocktail Wiener's 36
Cold Shoulder, Hot Catfish 82
Corn off the Wagon 201
Crab Stuffed Popper Cherry Tomatoes 37
Crabby Chicks 108
Crazy About Her Clam and Linguine 168
Crème de la Femmes Salmon 138

D
Dick Likes It Creamy Caesar Salad Dressing 22
Dick's Bread n' Butter 38
Dicks Cheater Garlic Butter 23
Dicks Garlic Croutons 28
Dick's Own Barbecue Salad 204
Dick's Tzatziki Sauce 24
Dirty Girl Rice 205

E
Ears Like Cauliflower Casserole 206

F
Feeling Smothered Pasta 84
Fishing for Compliments 110
Flex Your Mussels 140
French Guy Meat Pie 170
French Liqueur Chicken 112
Fromage et Deux Jumbo Shells 142
Fromage et Trois Spinach Dip 40
Fruit of Their Loins Grilled Halibut & Mango Salsa 172
Fuhgeddaboudit Prime Rib 144

G
Gobble It Up Turkey Casserole 174
Gold Digger Scalloped Potatoes 208
Good Shit Baked Brie 42

H
Hide the Salami Baked Chicken 146
Honey I'm Home Pork Chops 148
Hot Chick Salad 136
Hot Mama Melts 61

I
I'm a Catch Chicken Marsala 114
I'm Really Not a Jackass Jambalaya 176
I'm The Man Hamburgers with Sautéed Onions . 44
It's Not Me, It's You Meatloaf 86

J
Jacked Meat 130
Jerk-Off Chicken 88

K

Keeping It Wrapped Grilled Jumbo Shrimp 180

L

Let Her Down Easy Eggplant Parmesan 90

Love Slugs 46

M

Man Up Sausage Manicotti 150

Manly Macaroni Salad 210

Marg Or Rita Chicken 116

Mari-Me-Nara Spaghetti with Meatballs and Sausage 152

Meet the Chief Beef Stroganoff with Bacon 182

Mojo-Mojito Shrimp 118

N

Nascar Nachos 48

Nice Rack...of Lamb 154

Nice Yams 212

O

On Tap Guiness Stew 120

One at a Time Ladies Lasagna 156

One Crazy Taco 92

P

Penniless Beef Tenderloin 164

Pigs and Popper's 50

Poker Pizza Dip 52

Pre-Nup Fried Zucchini 213

R

Real Men Do Cry French Onion Soup 54

Red Hot Red Pepper Soup 56

Reservoir Dogs Casserole 58

Rice Peel-Off 219

S

Seducer Sambuca Shrimp and Scallops ... 122

Seeing Red Potato Salad 214

She's Perfect Pesto Portabellas 60

She's So Sweet Potato Frites 216

ShishkaDicks 94

Single and Sexy Caesar Salad 62

Six Month Mari-Me-Nara Sauce 26

Sloppy Dicks 64

Slow Cooker Beef au Beer Sandwiches 124

Smokin' Gouda Dip 66

Splitsville Pea Soup 100

Stalker Soup 68

Stick a Fork In It Porchetta Roast 96

Sultry Sour Cream 29

T

Tap That Sea Bass 158

Teaser Tomato and Cucumber Salad 218

That's the Spirit Pork Tenderloin 126

The Super Bowl Cheese Fondue 70

Their Little Lamb Chops 184

Thighs of Rum & Coconut 128

Three Months Salary My Ass Salmon 192

Three Sheets to the Wind Chicken 188

Throw Me a Bone Bake 'n Barbecue Ribs 160

W

We're Better Off Friends Fettuccini 98

What a Ham 190

Who's Your Daddy Chicken Diablo 186

Wicked Wedges 220

Wine and Cheese Biscuits 221

Wingman 72

DICK'S NOTES

DICK'S NOTES

DICK'S NOTES

DICK'S NOTES

www.ingramcontent.com/pod-product-compliance
Lightning Source LLC
Chambersburg PA
CBHW042137290426
44110CB00002B/41